Assessment Guide

A Guide to the Fountas & Pinnell

Benchmark
Assessment
System **1**

Irene C. Fountas

Gay Su Pinnell

Heinemann
Portsmouth, NH

Heinemann
361 Hanover St.
Portsmouth, NH 03801-3912
www.heinemann.com

Offices and agents throughout the world.

Fountas & Pinnell Benchmark Assessment System 1
Assessment Guide

Andrew Swaine: Cover (left/right), 1 (middle/bottom), pages 4-7, 11 (middle),
28, 41 (bottom), 105 (bottom), 117 (top)
Mike Swendner: Cover (middle), 1 (top), 3, 9, 10, 11 (top/bottom), 41 (top/middle),
59, 105 (top/middle), 107, 117 (middle/bottom), and 161

ISBN-10: 0-325-01184-2
ISBN-13: 978-0-325-01184-4

Printed in China
4 5 6 7 8 NOR 15 14 13 12 11 10 09

Table of Contents

Table of Contents *(continued)*

About the *Fountas & Pinnell Benchmark Assessment System*

In this section, we provide background for benchmark assessment in general and its relationship to our work in particular. An overview of the Benchmark Assessment System components displays the file box and its contents and gives a brief description of all the parts of the System. Finally, we share ideas about how to prepare for an efficient assessment conference.

Introduction to the *Fountas & Pinnell Benchmark Assessment System*

A *benchmark* is a standard against which to measure something. In *Fountas & Pinnell Benchmark Assessment System 1,* the standard is set by the benchmark books a student reads aloud and talks about during the assessment conference. These books have been written, edited, and extensively field-tested to ensure that they reflect the characteristics of texts and the demands of texts on the reader at each specific Fountas & Pinnell level.

Fountas & Pinnell levels, created and refined as a teaching and assessment tool over the past twenty years, represent twenty-six points on a gradient of reading difficulty (see Figure 1). Each point on that gradient, from the easiest at level A to the most challenging at level Z, represents a small but significant increase in difficulty over the previous level. There are two benchmark books (a fiction and a nonfiction) for each of these levels from A–N in the Fountas & Pinnell Benchmark Assessment System. Following the Benchmark Assessment System's standardized assessment procedure, you use these leveled benchmark books to identify each student's reading levels. Benchmark results yield optimal levels for independent reading and instructional reading at one point in time. The results also provide information about the text level that will be too demanding to allow for effective learning by the student.

The Fountas & Pinnell Assessment System is administered during a one-on-one, student-teacher assessment conference. For about

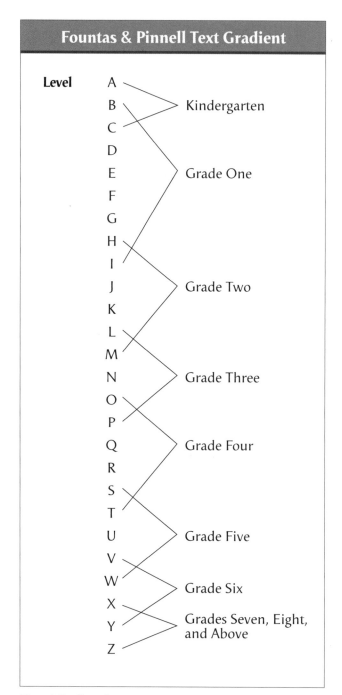

Figure 1. Gradient of text

twenty to thirty minutes, the student reads aloud and talks about a series of benchmark books while you observe and note the reader's behaviors on carefully constructed benchmark forms. Using established scoring conventions and procedures for analysis, you not only establish optimal learning levels but also gather valuable information about each individual's reading processing, fluency, and comprehension—all of which give you insights about how to target your teaching. Optional diagnostic assessments that focus on phonics/word analysis and vocabulary provide even more data to inform high-quality instruction.

Administered *once*, the Fountas & Pinnell Benchmark Assessment System conferences provide information to help you

▶ determine three reading levels for each student: Benchmark Independent, Benchmark Instructional, and Recommended Placement

▶ group students for reading instruction

▶ select texts that will be productive for a student's instruction

▶ plan efficient and effective instruction

▶ identify students who need intervention and extra help

Administered *more than once* in a school year or across school years, the Fountas & Pinnell Benchmark Assessment System can do all of that *plus* document student progress across a school year and across grade levels. As readers progress through the levels, becoming increasingly expert readers, the A–Z gradient becomes a "ladder of progress."

There are two ways to preview the Fountas & Pinnell Benchmark Assessment System—by reading through this guide or by exploring the *Professional Development* DVD. You will also find helpful information at fountasandpinnellbenchmarkassessment.com.

Components of the Fountas & Pinnell Benchmark Assessment System

All components of the system are conveniently packaged in a sturdy box that includes hanging file folders for the purpose of organizing the benchmark books and Recording Forms by level for easy access.

Benchmark Assessment System

Benchmark Books

**Assessment
Guide**

*The Continuum
of Literacy
Learning,* K–2

**Assessment
Forms book**

**Optional Assessments:
Student Forms**

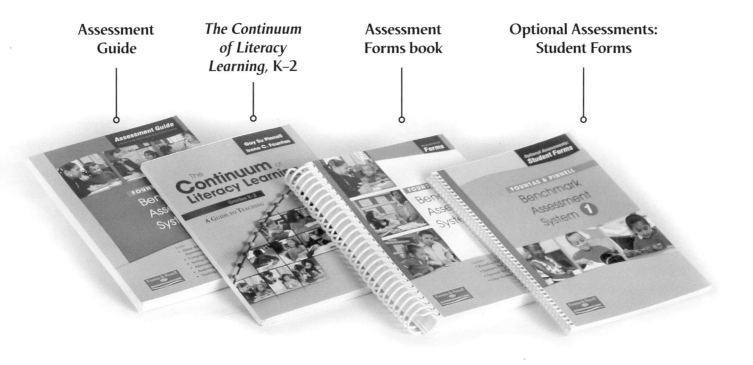

F & P Calculator / Stopwatch

Recording Forms

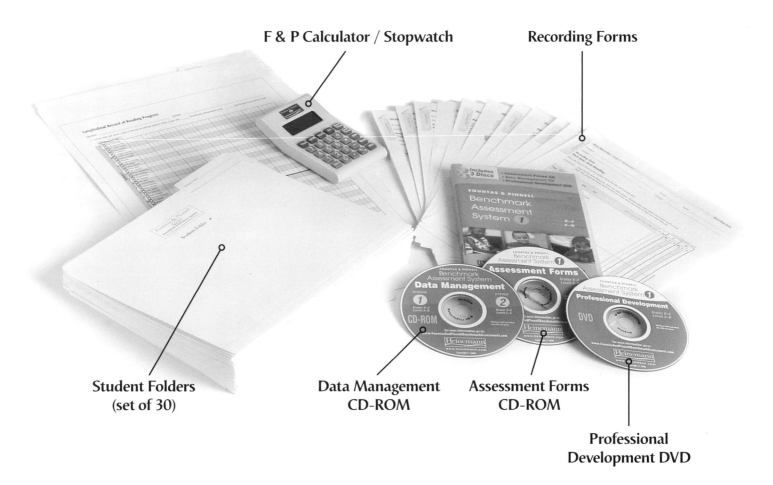

**Student Folders
(set of 30)**

**Data Management
CD-ROM**

**Assessment Forms
CD-ROM**

**Professional
Development DVD**

Benchmark Books

Twenty-eight benchmark books, a fiction and a nonfiction text for each level from A–N, are the centerpiece of the *Fountas & Pinnell Benchmark Assessment System 1*. Books are organized from lowest (A) to highest (N) level to reflect increasingly challenging texts. Each fiction and nonfiction book has been written to reflect the text characteristics specific to the level. (See *Leveled Books, K–8: Matching Texts to Readers for Effective Teaching* [Heinemann, 2006] for a full description of these level characteristics.) In addition, each benchmark book has been field-tested and edited to ensure representation of the designated level, whether fiction or nonfiction. Fiction and nonfiction pairs have been matched so that if a student can read one genre, he should be able to read the other at the same level.

The characteristics of all twenty-eight benchmark books in the *Fountas & Pinnell Benchmark Assessment System 1* are described in detail in Appendix A.

Assessment Forms Book and CD-ROM

All forms for the system are available in a book of blackline masters as well as in electronic form on a CD-ROM. Both the Forms book and the Forms CD-ROM contain resources that can be copied or printed in the quantities needed for assessment: Recording Forms and Assessment Summary forms, Class Record forms, Records of Reading Progress, At-a-Glance charts for easy administration, and optional assessments. On the CD-ROM, a simple navigation system allows you to select forms based on book level, title, and genre. An option is available to print out the Recording Forms in an enlarged font for easy legibility. Appendix B lists the contents of the *Assessment Forms* book and CD-ROM.

Professional Development DVD

The *Professional Development* DVD provides a foundation for understanding the Fountas & Pinnell Benchmark Assessment System materials and procedures. Its goal is to provide individualized training in coding, scoring, analyzing, and interpreting oral reading records and using the information to inform teaching. The DVD walks you through the parts of the program and the assessment administration procedures. It includes an overview of the program components, multiple models of real teachers administering the benchmark assessment with real students, as well as an in-depth discussion of scoring, analyzing, and interpreting an assessment. Practice sessions with sample assessment data provide you with opportunities to train yourself anywhere and any time on coding oral reading; scoring accuracy, fluency, and comprehension; analyzing and interpreting results; and documenting change over time. The modular structure and interactive design of the DVD allow you to direct your own learning and focus on areas of greatest interest or need.

F & P Calculator/ Stopwatch

A specially designed F & P Calculator/Stopwatch performs highly specific functions related to the system. Input start and end times, running words, number of errors and self-corrections, and the calculator will give you the reading time (Time button), reading rate in words per minute (WPM button), accuracy percentage (Accur.% button), and the self-correction ratio (SC button).

Optional Assessments: Student Forms

This book provides a reusable student copy of the Where-to-Start Word Test and selected optional assessments (Phonics and Word Analysis as well as Vocabulary Assessments). Turned to the appropriate assessment, it can be placed in front of the student for oral assessments. Each student page is coated for durability and arranged to make it easy for the reader to follow.

Student Folders

File folders designed to be used for each reader are not only a handy place to store recent assessment results and observations but also are printed with a Longitudinal Record of Reading Progress that can be passed from grade to grade, K–8.

Data Management CD-ROM

The *Data Management* CD-ROM enables you to manage benchmark assessment scores, analyze individual and group progress over time, and compare data from any component of the assessment within small groups or entire classes. The data are securely stored on a teacher's individual computer. The reports generated by the CD-ROM are customizable according to preferences set by the teacher and can be printed and shared with colleagues and administrators as needed. A district version of the data management software that allows longitudinal data tracking within and across schools will be available separately.

Preparing for a Benchmark Assessment Conference

Even before you begin getting ready to administer the assessment, you will want to think about when and where you'll want to conduct the one-on-one Fountas & Pinnell Benchmark Assessment System conference. If you are the student's literacy teacher, you are the ideal person to conduct the assessment as you will gain, firsthand, a rich set of information to inform your teaching.

Get Started Quickly

Plan to begin your assessment conferences right at the start of the school year and spend about two weeks of your daily reading block time completing them. The assessment conference will give you a chance to spend time with each student. Get to know your students and begin to develop relationships while you gather critical information. You can think of the assessment conference as time well spent on reading, thinking, and talking with students. You may also decide to have them do the writing portion of the assessment, giving them another opportunity to engage in a worthwhile literacy activity that provides evidence of text understanding.

Use Reading Block Time

We suggest that you conduct your assessment during your reading block times while the children are rotating to centers, reading independently, or engaged in other assigned independent literacy work. Plan to complete about two or three assessments per day. Some assessment conferences will be short, while others will be longer. This schedule will enable you to complete your series of assessment conferences in about two weeks.

Enlist School Support

You may have a teaching assistant, a student teacher, or a rotating substitute teacher in the school who might read aloud to the students, engage them in shared reading, or monitor independent work. This support will free you up to conduct two or three assessment conferences each day.

If your school is able to provide one or two days of substitute coverage, you will be able to assess most of your students quickly. The substitute can provide instruction while you work efficiently to take each of your students for an assessment conference.

Another option is to pair up with a grade-level colleague so that one of you can teach students from both classes while the other conducts assessments with his or her own students.

Select a Location

Find a place that is reasonably quiet to administer the assessment system. You will not want the child to be distracted and you also want to hear the child's responses clearly. Some specialist teachers have their own instructional space that is empty when they do not have students, so they can take the student to the room where it is very quiet. On the other hand, it may not be worth going a long distance down the hall.

We have had good experience with giving the assessment in a quiet corner of the classroom while other students are engaged in independent work. You may want to take this option (or work just outside the room in the corridor) if you have staff support. If you work in the classroom, you can have dedicated space in which you have your kit and all materials organized.

Be sure that you are conducting the assessment far enough away from the other students you are going to assess that they cannot hear the reading or conversation about the stories.

Put Materials in Order

The assessment will go more smoothly if you begin with everything prepared and in order.

▶ *Benchmark books.* Make sure the fiction and nonfiction benchmark books for each level are in the appropriate level folder in the benchmark kit. You can have the entire kit available (if you have space), or take out the levels that you plan to use.

▶ *Recording Forms.* Also in the hanging file folder, you will want to place multiple copies of all of the Recording Forms for both the fiction and the nonfiction benchmark books. These forms have the typed texts for each book and the space to record all

of your information. Printing out multiple copies from the *Assessment Forms* CD-ROM or copying them from the book and keeping them in good supply in the hanging folders will save time going to the printer or copy machine for each assessment.

▶ *Assessment Summary.* You will want to have a supply of these generic forms, also found in the *Assessment Forms* book and CD-ROM, in a folder in the front of your kit. You'll need at least one copy to summarize the set of text readings for each child you assess.

▶ *F & P Calculator/Stopwatch.* While you can do the assessment without the F & P Calculator/Stopwatch (using the formulas included on the Recording Form), it will be quicker and easier to have your F & P Calculator/Stopwatch with you.

▶ *At-a-Glance charts.* Two charts in the *Assessment Forms* book and CD-ROM will be helpful in reminding you of key steps in the assessment process. Make a copy of each to clip on your clipboard or laminate for your assessment corner. The Assessment at-a-Glance chart provides a concise description of the administration procedures. It will be helpful in reminding you of the steps, especially the first year you use the system. The Coding and Scoring at-a-Glance chart provides a quick review of coding and scoring procedures for oral reading. Over time, you will be so familiar with this information that you will not need to use the charts. (The At-a-Glance charts are also inside the covers of this book.)

▶ *Writing implements.* Have a good supply of writing implements—sharpened pencils or markers—so you will not have to spend time looking for them. We suggest that you use inexpensive mechanical pencils so you can erase if needed. If you choose to have students complete the optional drawing or writing section of the assessment, it will be more efficient to give the students a pencil or a fine marker rather than having them look for their own. A fine marker is ideal, allowing students to simply cross out when needed instead of spending time erasing.

Administering and Scoring the
Fountas & Pinnell Benchmark Assessment System

In this section, you will find directions for administering the Fountas & Pinnell Benchmark Assessment System. You can print a spare version of these directions (Assessment at-a-Glance) from the inside front cover or the *Assessment Forms* book or CD-ROM and place it in front of you as you conduct the assessment. You might want to copy it on card stock and laminate it or tape it in the area in which you conduct your assessment conferences. The *Professional Development* DVD offers additional guidance on how to administer, score, and analyze Benchmark Assessments.

We begin with a walk-through of the Recording Form, which is the System's primary tool for collecting and recording data about the child's oral reading and comprehension. Each book in the Fountas & Pinnell Benchmark Assessment System has a corresponding three-part Recording Form that guides the assessment procedures at all levels. It is used to observe and code the reading behavior through Oral Reading (Part One), a Comprehension Conversation (Part Two), and an optional Writing About Reading prompt for responding to the text (Part Three). The first four pages of this section present a brief summary of the form. A detailed explanation follows.

Recording Form Walk-Through

Part One: Oral Reading

The oral reading section of the assessment includes:

1 Space for the student's name, grade, the date of the assessment, the teacher's name, and the school's name. You'll have a Recording Form for each book a student reads.

2 A standardized text introduction to read aloud to the student after showing the child the benchmark book cover and reading aloud the title.

3 At levels J–N, a place to record the start and end time. You will use the reading time and the running words (RW) later to calculate reading rate, or use the F & P Calculator/Stopwatch.

4 The typed text of the benchmark book appears word for word, page for page. On this text, you code the oral reading, recording errors (repetitions, substitutions, omissions, insertions), self-corrections, appeals, and totals.

5 Columns to tally the reader's errors (E) and self-corrections (SC), with additional columns for analysis of these errors and self-corrections. Each of these attempts is analyzed for the source of information the reader likely used to make it: M = meaning, S = language structure, and V = visual information.

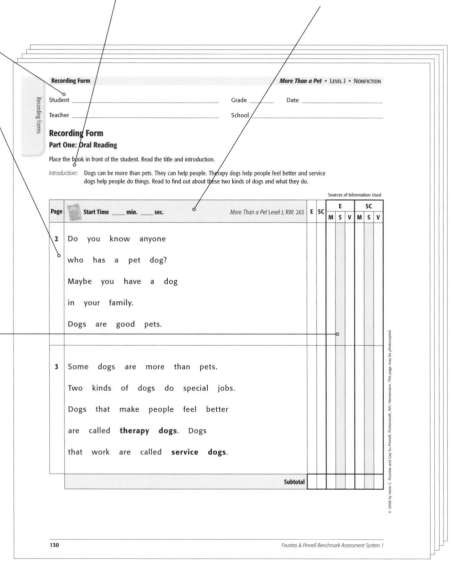

The scoring section summarizes the oral reading: accuracy, self-correction ratio, and fluency for all levels; reading rate for levels J and above.

6 A chart to help you quickly figure the accuracy rate (the percentage of the total words that the student has read correctly) by tallying the number of errors on the coded text and circling the errors and matching percentage on the scale.

7 A space to record the self-correction (when the reader makes an error and then, without help from the teacher, corrects it) ratio by adding the total errors and total self-corrections together and dividing by the number of self-corrections or by using the F & P Calculator/Stopwatch.

8 A four-point (0–3) fluency scale and scoring key for evaluating fluency (the way the reading sounds), including phrasing, intonation, pausing, stress, rate, and integration.

9 At levels J–N, a place to record the reading rate, the number of words per minute (WPM) the student read. The form provides the formula for calculating the reading rate or you can use the F & P Calculator/Stopwatch.

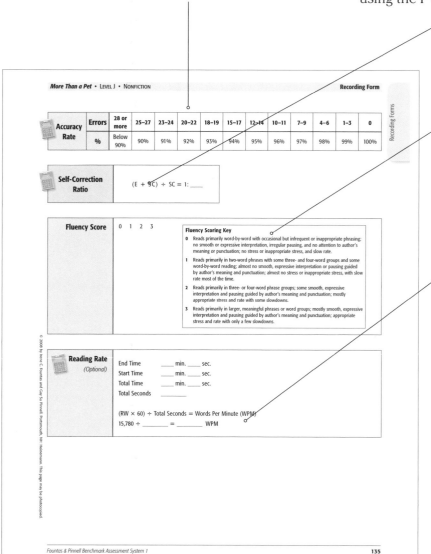

More Than a Pet • LEVEL J • NONFICTION   Recording Form

Accuracy Rate	Errors	28 or more	25–27	23–24	20–22	18–19	15–17	12–14	10–11	7–9	4–6	1–3	0
	%	Below 90%	90%	91%	92%	93%	94%	95%	96%	97%	98%	99%	100%

Self-Correction Ratio   (E + SC) ÷ SC = 1: _____

Fluency Score   0   1   2   3

Fluency Scoring Key

0 Reads primarily word-by-word with occasional but infrequent or inappropriate phrasing; no smooth or expressive interpretation, irregular pausing, and no attention to author's meaning or punctuation; no stress or inappropriate stress, and slow rate.

1 Reads primarily in two-word phrases with some three- and four-word groups and some word-by-word reading; almost no smooth, expressive interpretation or pausing guided by author's meaning and punctuation; almost no stress or inappropriate stress, with slow rate most of the time.

2 Reads primarily in three- or four-word phrase groups; some smooth, expressive interpretation and pausing guided by author's meaning and punctuation; mostly appropriate stress and rate with some slowdowns.

3 Reads primarily in larger, meaningful phrases or word groups; mostly smooth, expressive interpretation and pausing guided by author's meaning and punctuation; appropriate stress and rate with only a few slowdowns.

Reading Rate *(Optional)*
End Time   _____ min. _____ sec.
Start Time   _____ min. _____ sec.
Total Time   _____ min. _____ sec.
Total Seconds _____

(RW × 60) ÷ Total Seconds = Words Per Minute (WPM)
15,780 ÷ _____ = _____ WPM

Recording Form Walk-Through, *continued*

Part Two: Comprehension Conversation

Immediately after the oral reading, and before the scoring is complete, you will engage the reader in a comprehension conversation about the benchmark book.

10 An open-ended invitation to talk about the book.

11 A chart of key understandings, important ideas, or thinking that the reader should have gained from *within* the text (getting the literal meaning by processing words and stated ideas), *beyond* the text (getting the implied meaning and synthesizing information), and (at levels L–N) *about* the text (engaging in critical analysis and responding to the writer's craft). The chart includes space to write in additional understandings the student demonstrates.

12 The chart also includes a column containing prompts to help you elicit the key understandings (important ideas) the reader may not have mentioned.

13 A comprehension scoring key that will guide you in scoring each category of key understandings on a four-point (0–3) scale in the score column.

14 The guide to total score, used after totaling the category scores, helps to designate comprehension as excellent, satisfactory, limited, or unsatisfactory.

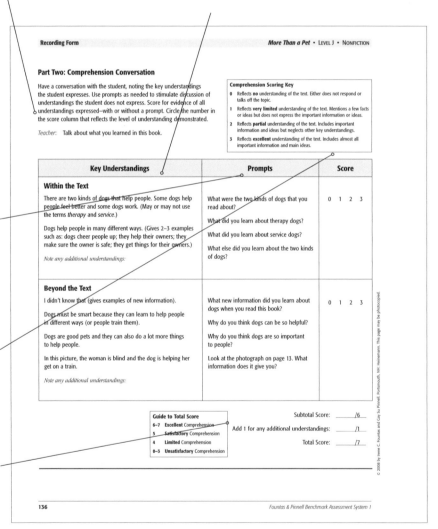

Recording Form — *More Than a Pet* • LEVEL J • NONFICTION

Part Two: Comprehension Conversation

Have a conversation with the student, noting the key understandings the student expresses. Use prompts as needed to stimulate discussion of understandings the student does not express. Score for evidence of all understandings expressed–with or without a prompt. Circle the number in the score column that reflects the level of understanding demonstrated.

Teacher: Talk about what you learned in this book.

Comprehension Scoring Key

0 Reflects **no** understanding of the text. Either does not respond or talks off the topic.

1 Reflects **very limited** understanding of the text. Mentions a few facts or ideas but does not express the important information or ideas.

2 Reflects **partial** understanding of the text. Includes important information and ideas but neglects other key understandings.

3 Reflects **excellent** understanding of the text. Includes almost all important information and main ideas.

Key Understandings	Prompts	Score
Within the Text There are two kinds of dogs that help people. Some dogs help people feel better and some dogs work. (May or may not use the terms *therapy* and *service*.) Dogs help people in many different ways. (Gives 2–3 examples such as: dogs cheer people up; they help their owners; they make sure the owner is safe; they get things for their owners.) *Note any additional understandings:*	What were the two kinds of dogs that you read about? What did you learn about therapy dogs? What did you learn about service dogs? What else did you learn about the two kinds of dogs?	0 1 2 3
Beyond the Text I didn't know that (gives examples of new information). Dogs must be smart because they can learn to help people in different ways (or people train them). Dogs are good pets and they can also do a lot more things to help people. In this picture, the woman is blind and the dog is helping her get on a train. *Note any additional understandings:*	What new information did you learn about dogs when you read this book? Why do you think dogs can be so helpful? Why do you think dogs are so important to people? Look at the photograph on page 13. What information does it give you?	0 1 2 3

Guide to Total Score

6–7 **Excellent** Comprehension
5 **Satisfactory** Comprehension
4 **Limited** Comprehension
0–3 **Unsatisfactory** Comprehension

Subtotal Score: _____ /6

Add 1 for any additional understandings: _____ /1

Total Score: _____ /7

© 2008 by Irene C. Fountas and Gay Su Pinnell. Portsmouth, NH: Heinemann. This page may be photocopied.

136 — *Fountas & Pinnell Benchmark Assessment System 1*

Part Three: Writing About Reading

15 A prompt for the (optional) writing/drawing assessment designed to provide additional evidence of text comprehension.

16 A four-point (0–3) scale for holistically scoring the writing about reading is provided on page 39 in this guide.

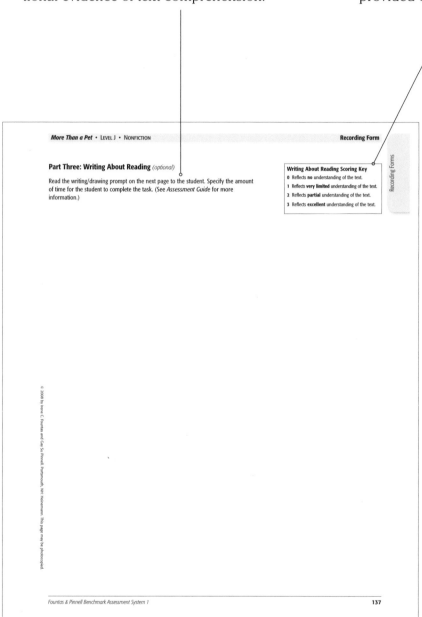

More Than a Pet • LEVEL J • NONFICTION   Recording Form

Part Three: Writing About Reading *(optional)*

Read the writing/drawing prompt on the next page to the student. Specify the amount of time for the student to complete the task. (See *Assessment Guide* for more information.)

Writing About Reading Scoring Key
0 Reflects **no** understanding of the text.
1 Reflects **very limited** understanding of the text.
2 Reflects **partial** understanding of the text.
3 Reflects **excellent** understanding of the text.

Recording Forms

Fountas & Pinnell Benchmark Assessment System 1   **137**

Finding a Place to Start

If you do not have sufficient information from the previous teacher or school records to judge the starting point for the assessment, you may want to use the Where-to-Start Word Test in the *Assessment Forms* book or CD-ROM. It is a series of lists of increasingly difficult words, organized by grade level and designed to help you approximate the starting point. One way to save time and still get excellent assessment data from benchmark testing is to find a good place to start.

You will always have the student read at least three texts as you determine the Benchmark Independent, Benchmark Instructional, and Recommended Placement levels for each child:

▶ *Easy text:* For levels A–K, a book is easy when the child can read it at 95–100% accuracy with excellent or satisfactory comprehension. For levels L–N, the expectation for accuracy is higher. An easy book is one that the child can read at 98–100% accuracy with excellent or satisfactory comprehension.

▶ *Instructional text:* For levels A–K, a book is in instructional range when it can be read at 90–94% accuracy with excellent or satisfactory comprehension *or* 95–100% accuracy with limited comprehension. For levels L–N, instructional range is 95–97% accuracy with excellent or satisfactory comprehension *or* 98–100% accuracy with limited comprehension.

▶ *Hard text:* For levels A–K, a book is hard when the child reads with below 90% accuracy with any comprehension score. A text read at 90–94% accuracy with limited comprehension is also hard. For levels L–N, a text is hard when read with below 95% accuracy with any comprehension score. A text read at 95–97% accuracy and limited comprehension is also hard.

Ideally, you will start the assessment on a level that is easy for the reader—that is, one that the child can read independently with 95–100% accuracy (A–K) or 98–100% accuracy (L–N). This text:

▶ is likely to support effective comprehension

▶ allows the reader to process smoothly and with phrasing

▶ allows the reader to start with success

If you have recorded an easy, or independent, level text for the reader, then continue the assessment with increasingly more difficult books (higher levels). You want to find the Benchmark Instructional level. Have the student continue to read until he reads with less than 90% accuracy for levels A–K or less than 95% accuracy for levels L–N with excellent or satisfactory comprehension. The number of errors (E) that places the child below 90% (A–K) or below 95% (L–N), the criterion for instructional level, is noted on the front of the book he is reading. When that happens, you should have three levels: (1) the highest level read independently, (2) the highest level read at an instructional level, and (3) the level that is too difficult for the student (hard text). *Then* you can make a decision about the recommended placement level—the best level for instructional reading.

We summarize the kinds of starting-point information you can use from two different kinds of literacy programs in Figure 2. If your students have been learning to read in a leveled books program, use column 1. If they are learning to read in a standard textbook program, you will want to refer to column 2.

If you are assessing the child at the beginning of the school year or when a child first enters your classroom, first consider information from last year's teacher and the student records. In Figure 2 we provide some thinking that will help you choose a place to start.

Sources of Information for Determining Assessment Starting Point (Independent Level)	
Leveled Books Program	**Core or Basal Program**
Use records or book charts from previous school year.	Use records from previous school year (see Figure 3 for conversion to Fountas and Pinnell level).
Identify books the student is reading independently (see *Fountas & Pinnell Leveled Book List, K–8* [Heinemann, 2006] or fountasandpinnellleveledbooks.com) for level, and start one level lower.	Identify books the student is reading independently (see *Fountas & Pinnell Leveled Book List* or fountasandpinnellleveledbooks.com) for level, and start one level lower.
Identify instructional-level books the student is reading in a reading group and start one level lower.	Identify instructional-level book the student is reading (see Figure 4 for conversion to Fountas & Pinnell levels).
Use Where-to-Start Word Test (*Assessment Forms* book and CD-ROM; *Optional Assessments: Student Forms* book).	Use Where-to-Start Word Test (*Assessment Forms* book and CD-ROM; *Optional Assessments: Student Forms* book).
For English language learners, consider any information you have on language proficiency assessments. Also, all of the above information will be helpful in determining where to start.	For English language learners, consider any information you have on language proficiency assessments. Also, all of the above information will be helpful in determining where to start.

Figure 2. Sources of information for determining assessment starting point

Remember that children are reading *unseen* text with only a minimal introduction to the text. The reading level they are able to achieve will give you a very good idea of the kind of texts they can read with teacher support. If you are working with an English language learner at the beginning of the year (or one who is new to the school), you may not have enough information about language proficiency to determine a place to start. Conversing with the student over several days and informally trying out a few leveled texts will provide more information. You will want to follow your district policy regarding language proficiency requirements and the administration of standardized tests prior to administering the Benchmark

Assessment System. We believe you will find the small, precise differences in the benchmark book levels very useful in gathering information about the reading skills of English language learners.

If you are assessing at the middle or end of the school year, one of the best sources of information about where to start comes from the student's current reading performance in the classroom. If you are the classroom teacher and you have worked with the student recently, then you probably have a good idea of his instructional level. If you are not the classroom teacher, you can ask for advice about the level the child is reading. Figure 3 shows how you might determine a starting level at the

Approximate Start Level Based on Expected Grade-Level Performance

Grade	Reading Performance (how the child is reading relative to expected grade-level performance)	Time of Year			Approximate Benchmark Assessment Starting Level
		Beg.	Mid.	End	
Kindergarten	Below level	X			Not applicable
	Below level		X		A
	Below level			X	A
	On level	X			Not applicable
	On level		X		A
	On level			X	B
	Above level	X			Not applicable
	Above level		X		B
	Above level			X	C–D
Grade 1	Below level	X			A
	Below level		X		B–C
	Below level			X	C–D
	On level	X			B–C
	On level		X		D–E
	On level			X	F–G
	Above level	X			C–D
	Above level		X		F–G
	Above level			X	J–K
Grade 2	Below level	X			D–E
	Below level		X		F–G
	Below level			X	H–I
	On level	X			G–H
	On level		X		I–J
	On level			X	K–L
	Above level	X			K–L
	Above level		X		M–N
	Above level			X	N–O

Figure 3. Approximate start level based on expected grade-level performance

beginning, middle, and end of the school year when the child's general reading performance is known.

If you are using a basal or core program, you can also use the chart in Figure 4 to help you decide where to start. It will be helpful to think about the level of the basal core text or anthology your students have completed successfully and its correspondence to the Fountas & Pinnell levels (see Figure 4).

You may also opt to use the Where-to-Start Word Test, which is described in Appendix B and found in the *Assessment Forms* book and CD-ROM. This word test gives you a quick way to identify a starting point.

After determining the starting level—the highest level at which you expect the student will read with relative ease—locate the appropriate books in the benchmark kit and make sure you have copies of the Recording Forms for books at the selected level and for the levels before and after it. The fiction and nonfiction texts for each level are listed in Figure 5 on the next page.

For each level, you have a fiction and a nonfiction text. The level of the book appears in two places on every book: (1) on the front cover in the lower left corner and (2) on the back cover in the lower left corner. This will help you easily locate the appropriate book for the levels you have chosen. The genre of the book (fiction or nonfiction) is printed under the level on the lower left corner of the back cover. Fiction and nonfiction pairs have been matched so that if a student can read one genre, he is likely to be able to read the other. We recommend that you vary the fiction and nonfiction texts as you move up the gradient during an assessment conference, so if you begin with the fiction title, move on to a nonfiction title at the next level tested. This will give you a picture of how the student is performing in both genres.

Using the Assessment at-a-Glance Chart

For a quick reference, we suggest you copy the Assessment at-a-Glance Chart on the inside cover of this book, or print it from the Assessment Forms CD. The following sections take you step-by-step through the assessment conference.

Basal Anthology or Core Text User's Guide for Assessment	
Last Basal/Core Level the Student Completed	**Approximate Fountas & Pinnell Level to Start Testing**
Kindergarten	A
Grade 1 pre-primer (1)	B
Grade 1 pre-primer (2)	B
Grade 1 pre-primer (3)	C
Grade 1 primer	D
Grade 1 late	E
Grade 2 early	G
Grade 2 late	K
Grade 3 early	L
Grade 3 late	N
Grade 4 early	O
Grade 4 late	Q
Grade 5 early	R
Grade 5 late	T
Grade 6 early	U
Grade 6 late	V
Grade 7–8	W

Figure 4. Basal or core text user's guide for assessment

Level	Fiction	Nonfiction
A	*Best Friends*	*At the Park*
B	*My Little Dog*	*Playing*
C	*Socks*	*Shopping*
D	*The Nice Little House*	*Our Teacher Mr. Brown*
E	*The Loose Tooth*	*The Zoo*
F	*Anna's New Glasses*	*From Nest to Bird*
G	*Bedtime for Nick*	*Bubbles*
H	*The Sleepover Party*	*Trucks*
I	*The Best Cat*	*All About Koalas*
J	*Our New Neighbors*	*More Than a Pet*
K	*Edwin's Haircut*	*Surprising Animal Senses*
L	*Dog Stories*	*Giants of the Sea*
M	*The Thing About Nathan*	*The Life of a Monarch Butterfly*
N	*The Big Snow*	*Exploring Caves*

Figure 5. Benchmark 1 books

Introducing the Benchmark Book

Read the title of the book. Then **read the standardized introduction** to the reader. The standardized introduction to the text is printed on the colored wave at the bottom of the front cover and on the Recording Form. The introductions were created and field-tested to give the reader a start on the book and to ensure that each child tested would begin with the same introductory material. For the assessment to be standardized, you will want to take care not to embellish the introduction or enter into any additional conversation with the student about the text.

If you are using the F & P Calculator/ Stopwatch, **enter the number of running words** (RW), which is printed on the book cover and the Recording Form. The number of running words is the exact number of words that the child reads orally. It does not include, for example, the title of the book, captions under pictures, or diagram labels. This number is used to calculate the percentage of accuracy with which the student has read and the reading rate, which is the words per minute. The back cover has the total running words (TRW). For most books, the TRW and the RW are the same.

Note the number of errors printed under the running words on the front cover. (See Figure 6.) It indicates the point at which the reader's accuracy has gone below 90% (A–K) or below 95% (L–N). When this happens, the text is probably too hard. Keeping track of the number of errors as a child reads will allow you

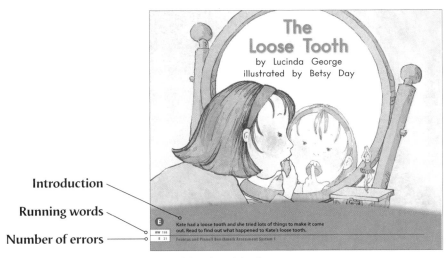

Introduction

Running words

Number of errors

Figure 6. Benchmark book cover

stopping point

Figure 7. Stopping point for oral reading

to switch to a lower level if the reader is having much difficulty. You will need to judge whether to have the student finish reading the book or whether you want to discontinue the reading.

Coding Oral Reading

Begin oral reading and timing. Start the timer on the F & P Calculator/ Stopwatch. Have the child begin to read the text orally. Alternatively, you can start your stopwatch or use a clock with a second hand and record the starting time on the Recording Form. Have the child read until the end of the

text (or to the stopping point, after which the child continues to read silently). At levels I–N, a stopping place is marked in the text (a black square) to show the point at which the student stops reading orally (see Figure 7).

The student reads orally up to the black square, or stopping point, while you code the behavior on the Recording Form. (Texts at lower levels do not have a stopping point since the student reads the whole text orally.) Then have the student continue to read silently. You can use this time to write comments and summarize the reading behavior.

Code the oral reading behavior on the Recording Form. The page number and typed text on the Recording Form correspond exactly to the benchmark book. There is space to record the student's reading behaviors using a standardized coding system. You will code what the student says above each word in the text. You can review each type of reading behavior and see examples of each in Figure 9 on the next page. (The *Professional Development* DVD provides simple and clear individualized training on how to listen for and code if you are not familiar and skilled with the process.) See Figure 8 for how one teacher's coding might look partway through one student's oral reading of *The Loose Tooth*.

Be sure to listen to how the reading sounds while you code errors, since you will simultaneously be evaluating accuracy (percentage of errors), judging fluency (the way the reading sounds), and using the timer to determine reading time. With especially fluent readers, you may get behind in your coding. If you get very far behind, you can ask the reader to stop and wait a moment at the end of a page. Or, if your coding is mixed up, you can ask the student to start over at a good point.

When the child has reached the end of the book or stopping point, **stop timing** and record the time on the form.

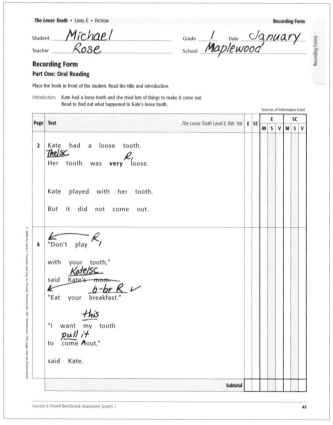

Figure 8. Coding oral reading of *The Loose Tooth*

	Coding		
Behavior	**What the Reader Does**	**Instruction**	**Code**
Accurate reading	Reads words correctly	Do not mark or place a check above words.	no mark or ✓Kate
Substitution	Gives an incorrect response	Write the substitution above the word.	her / Kate's
Multiple substitutions	Makes several attempts at a word	Write each of the substitutions in sequence above the word.	little|some|him / his
Self-correction	Corrects a previous error	Write the error above the word, followed by *SC*.	teeth |SC / tooth
Insertion	Adds a word that is not in the text	Write in the inserted word using a caret.	loose ∧
Omission	Gives no response to a word	Place a dash (–) above the word.	− / very
Repetition	Reads the same word again	Write *R* after the word.	✓R
Repeated repetitions	Reads the same word more than once	Write *R* for the first repetition, then write a number for the additional repetitions.	R 2 / R 3
Rereading	Returns to the beginning of a sentence or phrase to read it again	Write an *R* with an arrow back to the place where rereading began.	✓✓✓ R
Appeal	Verbally asks for help	Write *A* above the word.	A / very
"You try it"	Appeals and has not yet attempted a word; respond with "You try it."	Write *Y* after the word.	A / very|Y
Told	Tries the word and stops or asks for help; tell the child the word.	Write *T* after the word.	vē / very|T
	If you have said "You try it," but the child does not attempt it, tell the word.	Write *Y* after the word, then *T*.	A / very|Y|T
Spelling aloud	Spells the word by saying the names of letters	Write the letters in all capital letters with hyphens between them.	B-U-T / But
Sounding out	Makes the sounds associated with the letters in the word	Write the letters in lowercase with hyphens between them.	n-o-t / not

Figure 9. Coding conventions for oral reading

Coding system developed by Marie Clay as part of the running record system in
An Observation Survey of Early Literacy Achievement, Revised Second Edition, 2006, Heinemann.

Counting Errors to Get an Accuracy Score

Accuracy, the percentage of total words the student has read correctly, is only one indicator of a reader's ability to process a text, but it is an important one. It is an indicator of the student's ability to self-monitor or check on himself while reading. The amount of accurate reading is an important factor in supporting the student's comprehension and problem-solving while moving through the text. Children may read a text with high accuracy but understand it only superficially. They may read a text with lower accuracy but remember enough details to get the gist. But in general, there is a clear relationship between accuracy and understanding.

Since this is a standardized assessment, you will want to use established guidelines to count errors and assess all of your students in the same way. In fact, it is important for all teachers in a school and district to use the same system. Use the error-counting conventions in Figure 10 to standardize the assessment for all students so that progress can be accurately documented. The chart shows the conventions and how to look at each behavior to count errors and self-corrections.

Special Cases

▷ If the child skips a full page of print, intervene and tell him to read the page. Do not count this as an error.

▷ If the child inserts many words, you could have more errors than the running words on a page. This is likely to happen only at the lower levels. In this case, score the page as having the same number of errors as words on the page.

▷ Occasionally, especially at the lower levels, a child will begin to "invent" text, that is, tell the story by making up his own language, disregarding the print. If this happens, write *inventing* at the top of the sheet and stop the assessment. In this case, the text is below the accuracy criterion, or a hard text.

▷ When a reader is processing the text satisfactorily but gets mixed up and loses the place, just ask the child to start over at a good starting point and begin your coding again. Do not count this as an error.

▷ If you are using this assessment with a child who is an English language learner, you will need to be sure that the student speaks English well enough to understand the directions and the introduction, enter into conversation with you, process the print, and understand the text. Estimate the level and move down if necessary. If the child seems confused, read the introduction again. You can also paraphrase directions as well as the comprehension conversation to support greater understanding.

Errors and Self-Corrections

Behavior	Coding	Error Counting
Accurate reading	no mark or K̲a̲t̲e̲ ✓	No error
Substitution, not corrected	her̲ / Kate	One error
Substitution, self-corrected	Kate's̲ / teeth /SC / tooth	No error; one SC
Multiple substitutions, not corrected	little/some/him / his	One error per word in text
Missing the same word several times in a text	teeth̲ / tooth	One error each time missed
Errors on names and proper nouns—repeated during the reading	Kathy̲ / Kate Kelly̲ / Kate	One error the first time; no error after that, even if different substitutions are made for the nouns
Contractions (reads as two words or reads two words as contraction)	It's̲ / It is Do not̲ / Don't	One error
Multiple substitutions, self-corrected	little/some/him /SC / his	No error; one SC
Insertion of a word	✓ loose ✓ ∧	One error per word inserted
Omission of a word	✓ v̄e̲r̲y̲ ✓	One error per word
Skipping a line	at̲ school̲	One error per word
Repetition	✓R	No error
"You try it" followed by child reading correctly	A | | ✓ / wiggled | Y |	No error
"You try it" followed by a substitution	A | | wobble / wiggled | Y |	One error
"You try it" followed by a Told	A | | T / wiggled | Y |	One error
Told (teacher supplied word)	| T / wiggled |	One error
"Sounding out" followed by correct response	w-ig ✓ / wiggled	No error; no SC
"Sounding out" followed by incorrect response	w-ig | wobble / wiggled	One error
Sounding the first letter and then saying the word correctly	br ✓ / brushed f ✓ / fall	No error; no SC
Sounding the first letter incorrectly and then saying the word correctly	f | SC / come	No error; one SC

Figure 10. Error and self-correction convention

Coding system developed by Marie Clay as part of the running record system in
An Observation Survey of Early Literacy Achievement, Revised Second Edition, 2006, Heinemann.

Total the errors and self-corrections in each line of text separately. A self-correction is *not* an error. Then count the errors by going down the column (see Figure 11).

Next, **figure out the accuracy score**. Enter the number of errors and self-corrections on the calculator and tap the accuracy button to get the percentage of words read accurately. Alternatively, on each Recording Form, you will find an accuracy graph (see Figure 12). This graph will help you instantly calculate the accuracy. Just count the errors and circle the accuracy that is relevant.

If the student is reading below 90% accuracy (levels A–K) or 95% accuracy (levels L–N), you will want to consider whether or not to continue with the comprehension conversation. If accuracy is close to the criterion (but below it) and there are repeated errors, the child may have understood enough that the comprehension conversation will provide important information. However, if the accuracy rate is well below the criterion and the student had much difficulty, you will want to end the assessment.

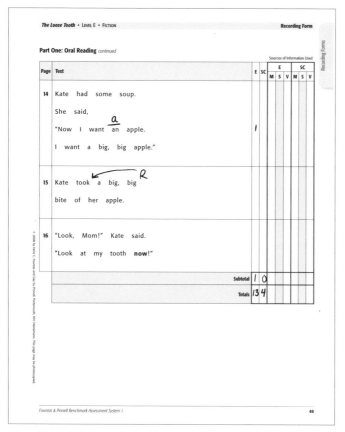

Figure 11. Counting errors and self-corrections

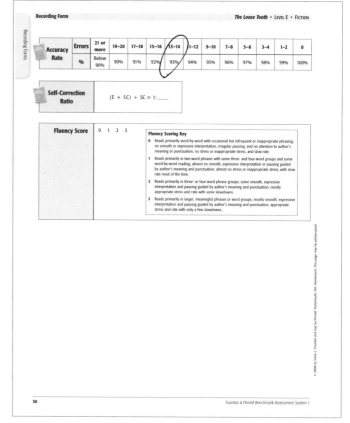

Figure 12. Accuracy score

Evaluating Fluency

Immediately after the student finishes reading orally at level C and above (not levels A and B), **rate fluency** by making a note at the bottom of the coded text of how the reading sounded, and circle the rating on the fluency scoring key. The fluency score reflects how consistently students are interpreting the meaning of the text through their voices. When reading at the independent or instructional level, students should read along at a reasonable pace. At the instructional level, you can expect fluent, phrased reading, though at the independent level, reading will be more consistently fluent throughout the text. Use the following guidelines to rate readers' fluency. A high score indicates that the reader is

▶ phrasing, or grouping words, as evident through intonation, stress, and pauses as well as through emphasizing the beginnings and endings of phrases by rise and fall of pitch or by pausing

▶ adhering to the author's syntax or sentence structure, reflecting their comprehension of the language

▶ expressive; the student's reading reflects feeling, anticipation, and character development

▶ using punctuation to cue pausing, or altering the voice

A simple four-point (0–3) fluency scoring key is included on the form and shown in Figure 13. Score fluency from 0 to 3 according to this key. (An optional, expanded Six Dimensions Fluency Rubric is included in the *Assessment Forms* book and CD-ROM.)

For reliable assessment across your school or district, view the examples of oral readings on the *Professional Development* DVD with a group of colleagues. Reach agreement on typical examples of ratings and then check with the ratings we have given. Once your group

has built an internal sense of what each rating means, you can quickly write down a rating for each record. Remember that the rating is not a label for an individual reader. It evaluates a single reading of a particular text.

Fluency Scoring Key

0 Reads primarily word-by-word with occasional but infrequent or inappropriate phrasing; no smooth or expressive interpretation, irregular pausing, and no attention to author's meaning or punctuation; no stress or inappropriate stress, and slow rate.

1 Reads primarily in two-word phrases with some three- and four-word groups and some word-by-word reading; almost no smooth, expressive interpretation or pausing guided by author's meaning and punctuation; almost no stress or inappropriate stress, with slow rate most of the time.

2 Reads primarily in three- or four-word phrase groups; some smooth, expressive interpretation and pausing guided by author's meaning and punctuation; mostly appropriate stress and rate with some slowdowns.

3 Reads primarily in larger, meaningful phrases or word groups; mostly smooth, expressive interpretation and pausing, guided by author's meaning and punctuation; appropriate stress and rate with only a few slowdowns.

Figure 13. Benchmark Assessment System fluency scoring key

Typically, a reader will demonstrate fluency and phrasing on texts that are easier (a score of 3). On more challenging texts, the same reader will slow down occasionally for problem solving but become more fluent on easier stretches of text (a score of 2). On texts that are too hard for the reader, the process will break down so that it sounds dysfluent most of the time (a score of 1). There are some readers, however, who have developed a habit of very slow reading. These readers may read with high accuracy but get low scores for fluency (a score of 0 or 1). On the other hand, some readers may gloss over errors or make careless errors, sounding fluent (a score of 3) but reading with low accuracy (80–85%). Each of these readers needs different instruction. Your diagnosis of a reader's fluency, viewed from the perspective of accuracy and comprehension scores, will provide information to inform teaching. Think about the reading as a whole, and make a judgment as to the extent it was fluent and phrased. Remember that on an instructional-level text, the reader may slow down to problem solve and then speed up again.

Fluency and English Language Learners

It is important to note that when they read orally, many English language learners will not sound precisely the same as native speakers of the language. The cadence of the reading may vary slightly, or different words may be stressed. There may be pauses to search for the meaning of an English word or to translate meaning into the individual's first language. Phonetic variations that do not interfere greatly with comprehension or fluency can be ignored. Make a judgment based on your knowledge of the student and your conversation with him.

Also, it is good to remember that sometimes an individual may sound fluent when reading in a new language because she has learned to decode the words. You will want to check understanding very carefully. Just because a reader can decode the words and read with a fair amount of fluency does not guarantee

understanding, and that is true of all learners.

Fluency and Early Levels

We offer a word of caution about students who are reading levels A and B. On these levels, you want children to point under each word as they are learning to match one spoken word with one written word. You are looking at their ability to read word by word to gain control over one-to-one matching and left-to-right directionality. You do not want to require fluent reading. Rather, you want children to slow down their oral language so they can use the black marks and white spaces in the text to help them match what they say with where they are looking. Inevitably, the reading will sound word by word and choppy. As the eyes begin to take over the process (at about level C) and early reading behaviors are firmly established, the reading will become faster and you will hear some phrasing and stress on particular words. At levels A and B, remember to make notes about how precisely the reader points under each word as she reads these early texts (see Figure 14).

Figure 14. One-to-one matching

Guiding the Comprehension Conversation

Often comprehension is assessed by asking the student a series of questions and checking the answers with a guide. Too often this can lead to students' thinking that they read to be able to answer the teacher's questions. For this assessment system, we have constructed a different process, one that will let you gather evidence of comprehension while engaging the child in a conversation about the text. As much as possible, the assessment activities should represent a reading conference. The student reads texts, converses with you about them, and then may do some writing about the text. As a general rule, you will want to complete the comprehension conversation on an easy, instructional-level, and hard text. However, you may decide not to complete the comprehension conversation if the text is much too hard for the reader, as you have strong evidence that the student did not likely understand it.

The Recording Form for each benchmark book provides a list of key understandings in the text, prompts that parallel those key understandings, and a score range (see Figure 15) for each type of thinking.

Understandings are categorized as:

▶ Evidence that the reader is thinking *within* the text. The reader is gaining the literal meaning of the text through solving the words, monitoring his own understanding and accuracy, searching for and using information, remembering information in summary form, adjusting for purpose and type of text, and sustaining fluent reading.

▶ Evidence that the reader is thinking *beyond* the text. The reader is making predictions; making connections with prior knowledge, personal experience, and other texts; inferring what is implied but not stated; and

synthesizing new information by changing his own ideas.

▶ Evidence that the reader is thinking *about* the text. The reader is thinking about the literary elements of the text, recognizing elements of the writer's craft, and thinking critically about the text.

Key understandings for levels A–K focus on thinking within and beyond the text. For levels L–N, key understandings address all three areas of thinking.

Once the student has completed the oral reading and you have determined that the text was not too difficult, **read the teacher's conversation starter** on the Recording Form to begin the conversation: "Talk about what happened in this story" or "Talk about what you learned in this book." The idea is to open a conversation that will allow you to see what the text has prompted the student to think. Be sure

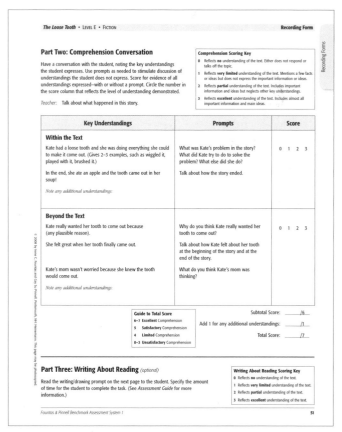

Figure 15. The Loose Tooth comprehension conversation

the child understands that he is expected to talk; some readers may think they are simply to listen or answer questions. Use conversational language to facilitate expansion of the child's talk. For example:

> ▶ "Say more about that."
>
> ▶ "What else?"
>
> ▶ "Can you talk more about that?"
>
> ▶ "What do you think about that?
>
> ▶ "Say more about your thinking."
>
> ▶ "Say more."
>
> ▶ "Tell more about that."
>
> ▶ "Why do you think that?"
>
> ▶ "And then … ?"
>
> ▶ "And then what happened?"
>
> ▶ "And …"

Often, just pausing a few seconds more to listen will also prompt the child to say more. Too often we don't give the students enough wait time to formulate a response.

Note: It is acceptable for readers to search back in the written texts for answers to prompts and questions if they initiate the action. Leave the book in front of the reader and allow him to use the text, but don't make the suggestion. Also, if a student reads the text orally to respond, ask him not to read from the book but to tell his answer in his own words.

As you listen and interact, you will find evidence of many of the key understandings. **Place a check next to the key understandings** in the left column as the evidence occurs in conversation (see Figure 16). Remember that you are not looking for word-for-word repetition of the understanding but rather for an indication that the reader understands the key idea. As you work with the Benchmark System, you will find it easy to detect specific evidence of understandings. If during your comprehen-

sion conversation a child discusses insights and information that are not reflected in the key understandings on the form, **jot down additional understandings** the student volunteers. You can evaluate them later as part of the scoring.

If the reader does not mention some of the key understandings on his own, **use the prompts** in the middle column to probe further. You can ask questions or ask the child to talk more about a topic to elicit evidence of understanding and check it off on the form. You can paraphrase the questions if needed. Do not judge the student's response lower because you have to prompt for thinking. Prompted responses are just as correct as spontaneous ones. If the student is able to articulate thinking, consider its value whether prompted or not. At the same time, avoid "leading" the student to an answer. Just use the prompt in a conversational way and move on if the student cannot respond.

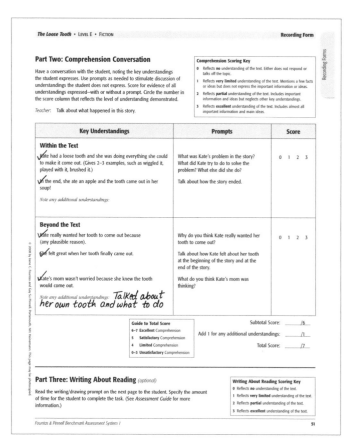

Figure 16. Recording evidence during the comprehension conversation

As you engage in this process with English language learners, make an extra effort to draw them into conversation, always realizing that the reader may understand more than she is able to explain in English. If you understand some of the student's own language, it is a great idea to converse for a few minutes using that language. But that is not always possible given the multitude of languages in our schools. Sketching may be helpful to the English language learner in expressing understandings. Also, time to write about the text may be easier for some students than talking immediately after reading. You can consider the student's sketching and writing in making a final decision about comprehension.

Scoring the Comprehension Conversation

After the comprehension conversation, **use the comprehension scoring key** (Figure 17) to judge the degree to which the student has demonstrated understanding of the text's key ideas and circle the appropriate number for each category: within, beyond, and about. This scale is not designed to "count" answers to questions in each category. Instead, make an overall judgment using the evidence in each of the three broad areas as to whether the reader showed unsatisfactory, limited, satisfactory, or excellent understanding of the information. Notice the Comprehension Scoring Key (Figure 17) that appears on the Recording Form, to guide your scoring.

Comprehension Scoring Key

0 Reflects unsatisfactory understanding of the text. Either does not respond or talks off the topic.

1 Reflects limited understanding of the text. Mentions a few facts or ideas but does not express the important information or ideas.

2 Reflects satisfactory understanding of the text. Includes important information and ideas but neglects other key understandings.

3 Reflects excellent understanding of the text. Includes almost all important information and main ideas.

Figure 17. Comprehension scoring key

As you circle the scores on the rubric, be sure that you have clear evidence of student understanding. Remember that this score will be an important indicator of the kind of teaching that you need to do later.

Then **score additional understandings**. Comprehension is such an individual factor that it is difficult to list the exact understandings that every reader should have. After analyzing the text, we provide the basic understandings that we think every reader should have; but each of us may actually take something different from a text based on our own life experiences. If your reader came up with one or more unique and valuable additional understandings, add a point to the comprehension score.

Finally, add up the subscores and **use the guide to total score** to determine if the student's overall understanding was excellent, satisfactory, limited, or unsatisfactory (see Figure 18).

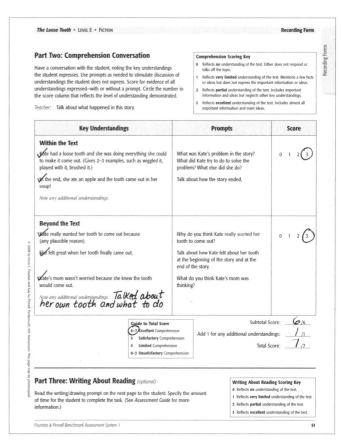

Figure 18. A scored comprehension conversation

Making the Most of the Comprehension Conversation

After practicing a few of these comprehension conversations, you will find that the process is both easy and enjoyable. They are similar to the kinds of conversations you have every day with children in reading groups or reading conferences. Over time, your students will learn how to spontaneously offer their thinking about a text—and that is a valuable strategy to have.

What is a conversation like? If we observed you and a friend, we would likely see something like this:

1 You say something.

2 Your friend comments on what you said.

3 You add more.

4 Your friend asks a question.

5 You answer and make another comment.

6 Your friend says more.

We contrast this scene to a series of continuous questions that are asked one after another. The point is that real conversation does involve some questions but not a steady barrage. The conversation is a flow of talk, back and forth.

Try to engage the student in showing her thinking about the text. We have suggested open-ended prompts like "Say more about that" to invite the student to talk more about what she understood. You may also want to use a specific question. Figure 19 summarizes some of these ways.

In Figures 20 and 21, you will see two examples of comprehension conversations with headings that explain what the teacher is doing and the scoring the teacher did using the evidence the student provided in discussion.

Ways to Have a Good Comprehension Conversation

▷ Be sure you have read and thought about the information in the book. If you know the text well, you can discuss it better. (The *benchmark books* text characteristics in *Appendix A* will help here.)

▷ Read the key understandings and prompts prior to the assessment so you are very familiar with them.

▷ Tell the student that you are going to be meeting with each one of them to listen to them read, so you will be able to help them as readers. Explain that you will ask them to read a short book and then you want them to tell all their thinking about what they read. Sometimes you will ask questions to help them talk more about the book, but you want them to do as much talking about the book as they can.

▷ Invite the student to share thinking and be sure to leave some silence before jumping in. It is very important to provide enough "wait time" for students, especially English language learners, to muster their thoughts and put them into words.

▷ Rephrase comments or prompt questions to be sure the student understands.

▷ Use open-ended probes such as "tell more," "say more," "why?" or "what else?"

▷ Think of different ways to ask the same question or get at the information.

▷ Allow the child to look back in the text if the child initiates it. If the student starts to read the book again, stop her by saying, "Just tell about the ideas in your own words."

▷ Use an encouraging tone when inviting the student to talk more.

Figure 19. Ways to have a good comprehension conversation

The Nice Little House—Level D	
Teacher - Student Interaction	**Teacher Scoring**
Gives initial prompt **T:** Talk about what happened first in this story. **S:** A horse went in the little house and then lots of other animals— a chicken and a cow and a skunk. They all went in the house. And then they didn't like the house. **Probes for more information** **T:** Then what happened? **S:** Then the skunk went in and they all ran away.	**Within the Text** 0 1 2 ③
Probes for more information **T:** Wow! Why did they do that? **S:** They were squished in the house and they ran away because the skunk was stinky. They were scared. **Uses a probing question** **T:** How do you think the skunk felt at the end? **S:** He liked the house 'cause now he can have a nice house and he isn't squished. **Probes further for underlying meaning** **T:** Why did the skunk call it a "nice big house" when all the other animals said it was a "nice little house"? **S:** He has the whole house and no other animals are there to squish him. **Probes further for inference** **T:** How did the skunk feel at the end? **S:** He was all happy and stuff 'cause he likes the house. He's smiling. **T:** He looks happy, doesn't he?	**Beyond the Text** 0 1 2 ③

Figure 20. Sample comprehension conversation, *The Nice Little House*

Giants of the Sea—Level L	
Teacher - Student Interaction	**Teacher Scoring**
Invites conversation **T:** Talk about what you learned in this book. **S:** Whales are very big animals, so big. And the baby whale is a calf. It eats so much that it gets big like the mother whale.	**Within the Text** 0 1 2 **(3)**
Probes further **T:** Can you say more? **S:** Whales sort of scream and they cry, sort of like singing to each other in the water.	
Asks a question to check for understanding of graphics **T:** Look at the photograph and drawing on pages 2 and 3. What did you learn from these pages? **S:** This is the real whale—the biggest one. And over here it shows that it is as big as 25 elephants put together. It's blue, too, but elephants aren't really blue.	
Probes further **T:** Did you learn anything else about whales? **S:** They breathe air through holes in their heads. They breathe air. A little whale is about like a baby horse. And they talk.	
Probes for inference **T:** Why do whales sing to each other? **S:** They tell each other how to find food and stuff and to know other whales are around.	**Beyond the Text** 0 1 2 **(3)**
Probes for comparison **T:** You said whales were a little like us. How are whales like people and how are they different? **S:** Well, they breathe air like people and they talk to each other kind of. But they live in water all the time and swim. Also, they eat raw stuff.	
Probes further to check for synthesizing **T:** What did you learn from this book that was new for you? **S:** Well, I didn't know about the talking to each other. And, I didn't know there were little whales, too.	

Figure 21. Sample comprehension conversation, *Giants of the Sea*

Continued on next page

Giants of the Sea—Level L	
Teacher - Student Interaction	**Teacher Scoring**
Asks for analysis of the writing **T:** Why do you think the writer included the photographs and drawings in the book? **S:** They help you see what whales really look like and their size and everything. **T:** Can you give me an example? **S:** This page (points to page 4) is where it shows you the different kinds of whales and over here (page 5) is where it shows you that the little one—the dwarf sperm whale—is just about like a pony. **Asks for comments on the writer's craft** **T:** Some whales are really big, aren't they? What did the writer of this book do to help you know just how big they are? **S:** There are the pictures and these little pictures of elephants. And he also says the whale is the largest animal on earth.	**About the Text** 0 1 2 ③

Figure 21. Sample comprehension conversation, *Giants of the Sea*

Selecting Books to Find Easy, Instructional, and Hard Texts

At this point you should have an accuracy score, a fluency rating, and a comprehension conversation score on the student's reading of at least one benchmark book. Take a look at these three scores.

If you started the assessment on a level that is easy for the reader—Benchmark Independent level—give the child a higher-level text for the next reading and have the student continue reading more difficult texts until the accuracy rate falls below 90% (A–K) or 95% (L–N) or the comprehension is unsatisfactory.

If you started with a hard text, you can simply move to a lower-level text until you find a text that the student can read independently (Benchmark Independent level) with satisfactory or excellent comprehension.

Your goal is to have the child read on three levels: (1) the student's Benchmark Instructional level, (2) his Benchmark Independent level, and (3) a hard text—the level that's too hard for him to read and understand.

Choosing the Writing About Reading Assessment

After you've finished assessing a student's oral reading, you may want to have her write to the prompt in part three of the Recording Form for one of the books she read, ideally for the instructional-level text. The writing is an optional part of the assessment. It provides additional evidence of the reader's understanding and a concrete sample of thinking that can go in the student's folder. The writing assessment is best completed immediately after the comprehension conversation, but the instructional-level text may not be the last one the student read. Allow her to look back at the book, but make sure she understands that she should write in her own words, not copy from the book.

There are some students who perform better if they have a chance to reflect and think about the text in the process of sketching and/or writing. They may reveal in writing greater understanding than they do in the initial conversation. On the other hand, some students have far better ability to talk about a text than to write about it. If the student has only sketched a picture, invite him to tell about it while you record the ideas. You will find that the writing prompt provides a very useful opportunity for your students to share their thinking through writing in a way similar to that required in standardized tests.

Read the directions to the student and answer any questions he may have. All of the writing about reading assessments include the option of sketching or drawing. You will want to help the students understand that they should make a quick sketch, not engage in a detailed drawing that takes a long time. Specify an amount of time for the writing and drawing. At the early levels (A–D), you will want to give up to ten minutes, while the middle levels may require up to fifteen minutes and later levels up to twenty minutes (see Figure 23). If you choose to specify different maximum time limits for each level of the writing assessment, be sure to be consistent with all students at the level.

Text Level	Recommended Maximum Time for Writing About Reading
A–D	Ten minutes
E–I	Fifteen minutes
J–N	Twenty minutes

Figure 23. Recommended writing about reading time

While writing or sketching, the student may look back in the text and may refer to examples from the text but should use his own words. Remember to tell the child, "You can look back at the book to check your ideas, but you need to tell your thinking in your own words." If you are working in the classroom, the students can complete this assignment as independent work, but you may want to ask them to work quietly at a location near you—but not so near that they can hear the content of your conversation. This will allow you to control the time they spend on the task and to ensure concentration. While one student is working on the written response, you can begin assessing the next student on your list or complete the scoring on the Recording Form.

Recording Form

Student __Michael__   *The Loose Tooth* · LEVEL E · FICTION   Date _____

Write about the three things Kate did to get her tooth to come out. You can draw a picture to go with your writing.

Kate kept on playing with her tooth. It was going to come out. So she could wriggle it It came out because she ate the apple

52   *Fountas & Pinnell Benchmark Assessment System 1*

Figure 22. Writing about reading prompt for *The Loose Tooth*

Finding Easy, Instructional, and Hard Texts	
If the first book is...	**Then...**
Easy **Levels A–K**: Student reads at 95–100% accuracy with excellent or satisfactory comprehension. **Levels L–N**: Student reads at 98–100% accuracy with excellent or satisfactory comprehension.	Move to a higher level text and repeat the same process until the student reads a text that is hard.
Instructional **Levels A–K**: Student reads at 90–94% accuracy with excellent or satisfactory comprehension *or* 95–100% accuracy with limited comprehension. **Levels L–N**: Student reads at 95–97% accuracy with excellent or satisfactory comprehension *or* 98–100% accuracy with limited comprehension.	Move to a lower level text and repeat the same process until the student reads a text that is easy and move to a higher level text until the student reads a text that is hard.
Hard **Levels A–K**: Student reads below 90% accuracy with any score on comprehension. **Levels L–N**: Student reads below 95% accuracy with any score on comprehension.	Move to a lower level text and repeat the same process until the student reads a text at an instructional level.

Figure 24. Finding easy, instructional, and hard texts

Continuing the Benchmark Assessment Conference

You have learned how to administer, code, and score a student's reading of one benchmark book. To complete the assessment conference, you want to gather more information about the student's ability to read easy, instructional, and hard texts. Your goal is to determine how the student reads all three types of text. The hard and easy texts help you identify the instructional text. You can use Figure 24 to help you find all three types of text to conclude the assessment conference.

Completing the Scoring on Each Recording Form

Before compiling the results of the benchmark assessment on the Assessment Summary form, you will want to complete any scoring you may not have done during administration. You should already have an oral reading accuracy rate, a general evaluation of fluency (for levels C–N only), and a comprehension conversation score. Calculating the self-correction ratio (for levels A–N) and reading rate (for levels J–N) and scoring writing about reading, if you chose to assign it, will provide additional information for decision making.

Calculating the Self-Correction Ratio

The self-correction ratio is a way to quantify the extent to which the student is monitoring or noticing errors in his own reading. If you are using the F & P Calculator/ Stopwatch, it will calculate this ratio for you. If not, add the total errors (E) and total self-corrections (SC) together and divide by the number of self-corrections to get the second digit in the ratio, 1:your number. That is, the reader self-corrected one of every [your number] errors (see Figure 25).

Calculating Reading Rate

Reading rate is a measure of how many words per minute a student reads. Rate is important because it is one indicator of the reader's ability to process with ease. When the reader processes the print at a satisfactory pace, he is more likely to be able to attend to the meaning of the text. He is also more likely to group

words as they are naturally spoken instead of reading one word at a time. It is possible for a reader to read individual words—one at a time—quickly, so it will be important for you to notice speed along with the other dimensions of fluency. Phrasing, or grouping words, is critical to effective processing of the text.

We suggest that you begin to calculate rate at level J, as students reading at about a beginning of grade 2 level have strong control of processing with longer texts, and the information will be more meaningful. At the lower levels, you will also consider rate as part of the fluency rating. You may choose to calculate rate at levels below J using the formula we provide or by using the F & P Calculator/Stopwatch.

If you used the F & P Calculator/ Stopwatch to time the reading, you need only enter the number of running words (RW) from the front cover of the benchmark book. The calculator will give you the WPM (words per minute) to record on the Recording Form. If you have used a clock or stopwatch, figure the total reading time in seconds and divide this into the number provided on the Recording Form to get the number of words read per minute (WPM). The chart in Figure 26 shows the expected oral reading rate for levels J–N as well as end-of-grade expectations.

Readers will develop individual styles for oral reading, so do not try to identify a precise reading rate that all must achieve. Use the chart in Figure 26 only to identify whether a student's reading is within a desired range. Remember that rate is a good indicator *only* if the student is reading a text that is not too difficult. On hard texts, all readers will read more slowly. Also, be sure to remember that all the dimensions of fluent reading (see page 27) are as important as rate. Reading rate is only one aspect of integrated and orchestrated processing of text.

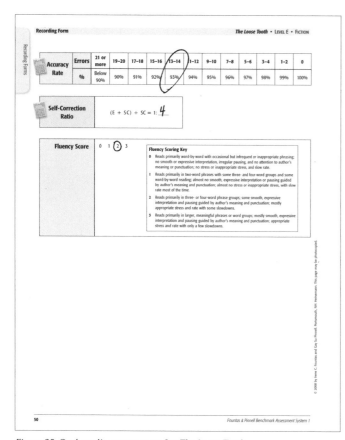

Figure 25. Oral reading score page for *The Loose Tooth*

Current Instructional Level	Oral Reading Rate (WPM)	Approximate End-of-Grade Expectations for Reading Rate (WPM)
Levels J–K	80–100	End Grade 1 Mid-Grade 2
Levels L–N	90–120	End Grade 2 Beginning Grade 3

Figure 26. Expected oral reading rates at instructional levels

Scoring the Writing-About-Reading Assessment

After the student has finished writing about reading, collect it for scoring. The purpose of this writing is to examine it for evidence of the student's understanding of the instructional-level text, so you will not be scoring it for conventions or craft, although you may want to notice the student's use of these. Look at the ideas that the writing reflects and assign a score using the guide shown in Figure 27. The writing-about-reading scoring key on your Recording Form is an abbreviated version of this rubric.

When Michael wrote about *The Loose Tooth*, his writing reflected excellent understanding of the text (see Figure 22), so the teacher gave it a score of 3.

Scoring Key		Rubric
0	Reflects **no** understanding of the text	The writing is not connected with text or is connected only in a very peripheral way (for example, about the same topic). The student's writing does not reflect any of the information in the text (thinking within the text) or of thinking beyond or about the text.
1	Reflects **very limited** understanding of the text	The writing is connected with the text but reveals either very little understanding or confusion. The student's writing does not reflect thinking beyond or about the text.
2	Reflects **partial** understanding of the text	The writing provides evidence that the student understands the literal meaning of the text (within), including key understandings, and in addition, is thinking beyond the text. It is not necessary for the writing to "retell" the text, but examples from it may be used as evidence.
3	Reflects **excellent** understanding of the text	The writing provides evidence that the student not only understands the literal meaning of the text (within) but grasps the author's message and is thinking beyond and about the text. It is not necessary for the writing to "retell" the text, but summaries, quotes, or examples may be offered in support of points.

Figure 27. Rubric for scoring writing about reading

Choosing Optional Assessments

If your district requires particular assessments in the areas of phonics, word analysis, or vocabulary, the *Assessment Forms* book and CD-ROM provide a variety of optional assessments from which to choose depending on the local need. See Appendix B for a complete list of these assessments. In addition, a student's previous records or his oral reading performance on the Benchmark Assessment may suggest areas you want to explore further. A High-Frequency Word assessment, for example, may confirm your hypothesis that a beginning reader's fluency is due to her lack of automatic recognition of high-frequency words. A Vocabulary-in-Context assessment will provide insight into a reader's use of meaning cues.

Analyzing and Interpreting Results of the *Fountas & Pinnell Benchmark Assessment System*

In this section, you will find step-by-step instructions for using the Assessment Summary form to compile assessment results as well as guidance in determining implications for instruction. You'll be filling out an Assessment Summary form for each reader you have assessed.

The Assessment Summary form is a summary record of key information from each of the individual Recording Forms you used with a student. It includes results from multiple Recording Forms and so provides an overall snapshot of a child's reading at one point in time and summarizes the Benchmark Assessment conference. Information from the Assessment Summary can be entered into the *Data Management* CD-ROM for individual and group data analysis and reporting. The first two pages of the section present a walk-through of the form. A detailed explanation follows.

Assessment Summary Form Walk-Through

The Assessment Summary form contains

6 A benchmark results box at the top of the page to record the two benchmark levels you checked below and a Recommended Placement level.

1 Space at the top for student, grade, date, teacher, and school information

2 A place to list, from easiest to hardest, the titles, genres, and levels of books the student read during the assessment conference

3 Columns for transferring from the Recording Form all scores for the books read (up to five books)

4 Boxes to check for Benchmark Independent and Benchmark Instructional levels. Simply check the box next to the level that meets the accuracy and comprehension criteria.

5 Space at the bottom to record comments about specific reading behaviors you noticed during the assessment conference or observed in reviewing the scores, as well as any instructional implications the assessment data may suggest

---

Summary Forms

Benchmark Independent Level* _____
Benchmark Instructional Level** _____
Recommended Placement Level _____

Student _____ Grade _____ Date _____

Teacher _____ School _____

Assessment Summary Form

List the titles read by the student from lowest to highest level.

Title	System 1 or 2	Fiction/Nonfiction	Level	Accuracy	Comprehension	Independent * (check one)	Instructional ** (check one)	Self-Correction	Fluency Levels C–Z	Rate Levels J–Z (optional)	Writing About Reading (optional)

*Independent Level:
Levels A–K: Highest level read with 95–100% accuracy and excellent or satisfactory comprehension.
Levels L–Z: Highest level read with 98–100% accuracy and excellent or satisfactory comprehension.

**Instructional Level
Levels A–K: Highest level read with 90–94% accuracy and excellent or satisfactory comprehension or 95–100% accuracy and limited comprehension.
Levels L–Z: Highest level read with 95–97% accuracy and excellent or satisfactory comprehension or 98–100% accuracy and limited comprehension.

Comprehension

Levels A–K		Levels L–Z	
6–7	Excellent	9–10	Excellent
5	Satisfactory	7–8	Satisfactory
4	Limited	5–6	Limited
0–3	Unsatisfactory	0–4	Unsatisfactory

Additional Comments:

Instructional Implications:

© 2008 by Irene C. Fountas and Gay Su Pinnell. Portsmouth, NH: Heinemann. This page may be photocopied.

Fountas & Pinnell Benchmark Assessment System 1   203

Benchmark Independent Level

The **Benchmark Independent** level is the highest level at which a student can read independently. The benchmark texts at this level are "easy" for the student. For levels **A–K**, the student can read 95–100% of the words accurately with excellent or satisfactory comprehension. For levels **L–N**, the student can read 98–100% of the words accurately with excellent or satisfactory comprehension.

Benchmark Instructional Level

The **Benchmark Instructional** level is the highest level at which a student can read with good opportunities for learning through teaching.

For the level to be instructional, one of the following should be true for levels **A–K**:

> The student can read 90–94% of the words accurately with excellent or satisfactory comprehension.

> The student can read 95–100% of the words accurately with limited comprehension.

For levels **L–N**, one of the following should be true:

> The student can read 95–97% of the words accurately with excellent or satisfactory comprehension.

> The student can read 98–100% of the words accurately with limited comprehension.

In all of these cases, word solving is sufficient but the student needs instruction to help him understand the texts at the level.

Recommended Placement Level

The **Recommended Placement** level is the level you decide is appropriate for reading instruction. It reflects your thinking about all of the data gathered during the assessment. Most of the time, this level will be the same as the Benchmark Instructional level, but sometimes a look at the reading behaviors and the specific data will lead you to a different decision.

Filling Out the Assessment Summary Form

Fill out an Assessment Summary form for each reader you have assessed. For each child, fill out the information at the top of the Assessment Summary form and organize Recording Forms for the books she read in order of the book level from lowest to highest text level. List the book titles, genres, and levels on the Assessment Summary form in this order. Then transfer from the Recording Forms to the Assessment Summary form the accuracy rate, comprehension score, and any other data you have figured on the reading of each book (see Figure 28).

Figure 28. Assessment Summary form

Finding Three Levels

Altogether, you will determine three different levels for each of your students: a benchmark independent level, a benchmark instructional level, and a recommended placement level. The first two are determined by the accuracy and comprehension scores you have already recorded. The third is determined by your careful analysis of the numbers and the quality of the child's processing.

First, look at the accuracy and comprehension scores you have recorded on the Assessment Summary form. Check the independent column next to the highest level at which a student can read at the criterion for accuracy with excellent or satisfactory comprehension. Check the instructional column next to the highest level at which a student can read:

▷ For Levels A–K: 90–94% of the words accurately with excellent or satisfactory comprehension *or* 95–100% of the words accurately with limited comprehension.

▷ For Levels L–N: 95–97% of the words accurately with excellent or satisfactory comprehension *or* 98–100% of the words accurately with limited comprehension.

The tables in Figures 29a and 29b provide a quick summary of the criteria for Benchmark Independent-level and Benchmark Instructional-level identification.

Finding the recommended placement level requires considering and interpreting these scores as well as looking across the rich range of information you gain from a benchmark assessment. In fact, no matter what the test is like, it always requires qualitative judgment on the part of a teacher. When you finish the benchmark assessment for an individual, you have an important set of numbers: (1) a percentage of words read accurately and (2) a comprehension score. You also have additional information on the reader's

- ▶ fluency in oral reading

- ▶ use of sources of information

- ▶ oral reading behaviors (errors, substitutions, self-corrections), or the way the reader processed the text

- ▶ ability to write about the meaning of the text

- ▶ control of early reading behaviors (levels A and B)

You can draw on all of these sources of information to help you look beyond the numbers and make a decision about a student's Recommended Placement level. The Recommended Placement level may be the same as the Benchmark Instructional level, but it may differ because of other factors that come out of your analysis. Look again at the accu-

racy and comprehension scores. Think beyond the categories and numbers you considered for benchmark levels to make a good decision regarding placement at a level for instruction.

Following are some general factors to think about when using data to select a recommended placement level for a student.

Actual Scores

Look at the actual scores rather than the categories only. While we have to establish "cut-offs" for logistic reasons, consider how close to the cutoff point a reader is. In real terms, there really is very little difference between 89 and 90%. However, it does make a difference whether the accuracy rate is 89 or 50% or whether the comprehension score is 4 or 0. These scores can make big differences and can figure into your placement decisions.

Benchmark Criteria for Levels A–K	Comprehension			
Accuracy	Excellent 6–7	Satisfactory 5	Limited 4	Unsatisfactory 0–3
95–100%	Independent	Independent	Instructional	Hard
90–94%	Instructional	Instructional	Hard	Hard
Below 90%	Hard	Hard	Hard	Hard

Figure 29a. Finding the benchmark levels, A–K

Benchmark Criteria for Levels L–N	Comprehension			
Accuracy	Excellent 9–10	Satisfactory 7–8	Limited 5–6	Unsatisfactory 0–4
98–100%	Independent	Independent	Instructional	Hard
95–97%	Instructional	Instructional	Hard	Hard
Below 95%	Hard	Hard	Hard	Hard

Figure 29b. Finding the benchmark levels, L–N

Fluency and Phrasing

Look at the student's fluency and phrasing. Some students read accurately but very slowly; slow reading generally interferes with comprehension. On the other hand, students may read fluently but carelessly, making many errors and losing comprehension. If a student reads a text with high accuracy but very slowly with almost no phrasing or recognition of the punctuation, then meaning will be affected. This kind of pattern suggests that you should teach intensively for fluency and phrasing at that level. Or you can move to an easier level for a short time if the other data indicate the level is too difficult for the student.

Text Content

Look at the content of the material. The student's background experience is a critical factor in comprehension. If a student has a great deal of background in an area, she may be able to answer questions or talk about the content even if the text is hard, so the comprehension score may be artificially high. Conversely, if the student lacks background knowledge or does not understand the culture in the text, the scores may be artificially low. The student may or may not be able to read other books at the level.

Sources of Information

Take a quick look at sources of information the reader used as she read the text: meaning [M], language structure [S], and visual information [V]. As you analyze errors and self-corrections, you can make hypotheses about the extent to which a reader is using different sources of information. For example, a student might read a text at an instructional level for accuracy but make substitutions that indicate use of the first letter of a word only without evidence of trying to make sense of a text. Another student might read the same text at just below an instructional-level accuracy but show effective use of word analysis strategies and good comprehension.

Problem-Solving Actions

Look at the reader's use of processing strategies or problem-solving actions. Observe to see if the reader makes several attempts or notices and corrects errors independently. Notice if the reader has a variety of ways to solve words. Think about whether these actions are effective and efficient. Some repeated errors signal a lack of self-monitoring, but they also can make the accuracy percentage artificially low.

Level of Independence

Look at the reader's independence in problem solving while reading the text. It makes a difference whether the student is actively problem solving or simply waiting to be told a word. For example, a student might read a text with high accuracy but stop and appeal at every unfamiliar word. This student is not demonstrating the ability to take risks and to actively search for and use information to solve words.

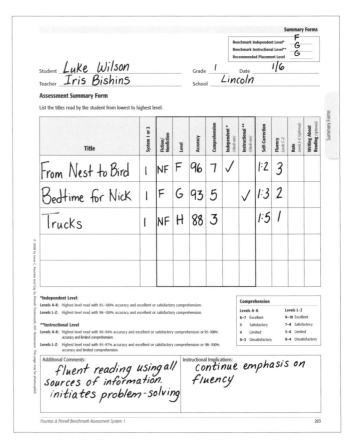

Figure 30. From Luke's Assessment Summary form

To make this decision-making process clearer, we provide examples and explanations of how additional considerations might influence reading placement levels (Figures 30–32).

Luke's benchmark scores (Figure 30) lead directly to his placement level. His benchmark scores fall neatly within the expected ranges. In Luke's case, his Recommended Placement level is the same as his Benchmark Instructional level. The teacher began the teaching at level G.

Although Gina's benchmark scores (Figure 31) suggest that she should be placed at level E, other factors contribute to the decision for a higher placement, at level F. Gina's score on level F was borderline, and Mr. Chavez felt that a few factors specific to the text dropped her score below the 90% level. To confirm his suspicion, Mr. Chavez had Gina read the next level (G). This was clearly too difficult but not dramatically different from level F. Mr. Chavez was confident that Gina should start at level F with teaching support.

Henry's benchmark scores (Figure 32) indicate level L placement, but his teacher has a rationale for placing him at level K. His Benchmark Instructional level is L (the highest level he read with 95% or better accuracy and satisfactory or excellent comprehension) but his teacher noted that his benchmark independent level was borderline (95% accuracy with satisfactory comprehension) and that he was not fluent. His teacher decided to drop down a level for a very short time and begin instruction at level K, knowing that Henry would gain fluency and firm up his processing strategies prior to moving to level L.

The box in the upper right corner of the Assessment Summary form provides a place to record all three levels.

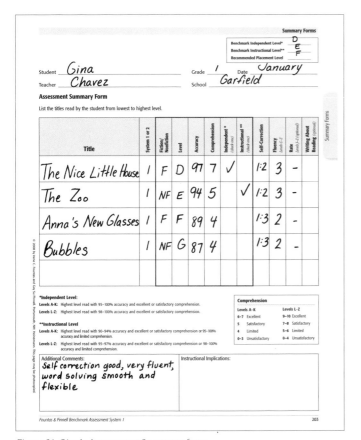

Figure 31. Gina's Assessment Summary form

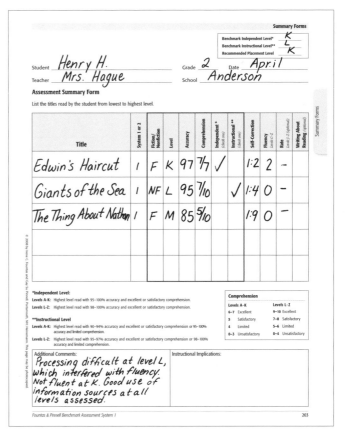

Figure 32. Henry's Assessment Summary form

Once you determine the student's Recommended Placement level, you can use the information to form guided reading groups and select texts for your lessons. Once you begin instruction and gain more evidence, you can always adjust the students' grouping if a placement is not working well.

In summary, the three levels you determine for each student are shown in Figure 33.

Determining Three Levels		
Three Levels	**Levels A–K**	**Levels L–N**
Benchmark Independent level	95–100% accuracy with excellent or satisfactory comprehension	98–100% accuracy with excellent or satisfactory comprehension
Benchmark Instructional level	90–94% accuracy with excellent or satisfactory comprehension *or* 95–100% accuracy with limited comprehension	95–97% accuracy with excellent or satisfactory comprehension *or* 98–100% accuracy with limited comprehension
Recommended Placement level	Best level for instruction after considering accuracy, comprehension, fluency, and processing strategies	

Figure 33. Determining benchmark and recommended placement levels

Solving Problems When the Numbers Do Not Match Up Perfectly

When you determine Benchmark Independent and Instructional levels, you are considering several variables rather than simply accuracy. It is worth the extra trouble it may take to look in this complex way because some students are extraordinarily competent as word solvers, but they do not think actively enough or they do not have enough background experience to understand what they are reading. There may be figurative language or big ideas that they do not understand. This kind of reading reveals strengths but does not add up to effective processing. In addition, it provides an unreliable view of the reader. A student who is "word calling" without understanding will not be able to function well on tests and will find it hard to learn from reading.

Occasionally, a student will read with low accuracy but be able to respond to questions—either from getting the gist of the story or from previously held background knowledge. This kind of reader may be merely careless about errors or have word solving difficulties that will affect future ability to process harder texts.

Because we have introduced a high criterion for accuracy as well as for comprehension, you may find that occasionally numbers do not exactly match the criteria for each of these levels. This situation will not be a problem when you are using the benchmark criteria for your own information and grouping. For example, you can have two independent levels (slightly different from each other) and then a hard text. You would simply make a decision on the placement level based on all the information and would not record an instructional level (or designate the harder independent level as close to instructional).

However, you may need to report two or three of the levels to the principal or the central office of your district. In this case, consult the chart in Figure 34. Here you will find some cases in which the numbers do not match neatly. The third column shows the teacher's solution to the problem. Find the one that most closely matches your own case and use it to help you make decisions about recording levels. After you have solved many of these problems, you will find that you can make these decisions quickly.

Finding the Instructional Level When the Numbers Do Not Match Up Perfectly

Problem	Example of student scores:	Solution
The student has 2+ independent levels and no instructional level.	H at 98% accuracy with excellent comprehension I at 98% accuracy with satisfactory comprehension J at 97% accuracy with limited comprehension K at 95% accuracy with unsatisfactory comprehension	Take the lowest independent level and make it the instructional level. If the next higher level is very close to 98%, use this as the placement level and expect the student to move quickly. I = Instructional level J = Independent level K = Recommended Placement level Remember that students reading at this level will *always* have many independent levels (all below the instructional level).
The student has 2 instructional levels.	J at 98% accuracy with excellent comprehension K at 95% accuracy with excellent comprehension L at 93% accuracy with satisfactory comprehension	Take the highest level instructional text J = Independent level K = Instructional level Expect this student to move quickly to level L as you work on word solving strategies.
The student has no instructional level because the reading is uneven.	C at 98% accuracy with satisfactory comprehension D at 93% accuracy with satisfactory comprehension E at 98% accuracy with satisfactory comprehension F at 90% accuracy with limited comprehension	For instruction, you want to be sure you are on firm ground. With uneven reading like this, select the level you are most sure that the student can process with your help. C = Independent level D = Instructional level
The student has no instructional level because of very high accuracy on one level, limited comprehension on the next highest level, and low accuracy and limited comprehension on the next.	F at 100% accuracy with satisfactory comprehension G at 99% accuracy with satisfactory comprehension H at 98% accuracy with unsatisfactory comprehension I at 75% accuracy with unsatisfactory comprehension	For instruction, use a text that the student can comprehend with your support. Even though the accuracy is very high, select level G and work on active thinking. F = Independent level G = Instructional level Expect the student to move quickly and monitor comprehension closely.

Figure 34. Finding the benchmark levels

Finding the Instructional Level When the Numbers Do Not Match Up Perfectly

Problem	Example of student scores:	Solution
The reader's comprehension is uneven, with unsatisfactory comprehension at a particular level.	D at 98% accuracy with satisfactory comprehension E at 95% accuracy with unsatisfactory comprehension F at 91% accuracy with satisfactory comprehension	You might want to try the alternate text at level E to see if the particular text had content that was unfamiliar to the student. Select F for instruction, but observe the reader closely and support comprehension. D = Independent level F = Instructional level
You do not have an independent level.	J at 98% accuracy with limited comprehension K at 92% accuracy with limited comprehension	You need to try lower levels to get a level the reader can process with satisfactory comprehension. J = Instructional level
You do not have an instructional level because there appears to be a large gap between two readings.	L at 99% accuracy with excellent comprehension M at 85% accuracy with limited comprehension N at 72% accuracy with limited comprehension	M is too hard for instructing this reader, and L is obviously an easy text. Try the reader on the alternate level M text just to check whether there is a particular difficulty with content. L = Independent level NA = Instructional level (not assessed) L = Recommended Placement level The student may read some books on level L as independent reading. Work to move the student quickly to M for instructional level.
All the texts seem too hard for the reader to understand.	C at 98% accuracy with unsatisfactory comprehension D at 100% accuracy with unsatisfactory comprehension E at 97% accuracy with unsatisfactory comprehension	You need to keep going down the levels until the reader finds a text that the reader can comprehend with limited comprehension (if 95–100% accuracy) or satisfactory or excellent comprehension (90–94% accuracy).
The student has no instructional level because all levels appear to be easy.	L at 98% accuracy with excellent comprehension M at 98% accuracy with satisfactory comprehension N at 98% accuracy with satisfactory comprehension	This is a good problem to have! If you have Benchmark 2 in your school, you may want to try levels O, P, and Q. Or you can identify level N as both Independent and Instructional. This student will benefit from small-group discussion, extending understanding through writing, and wide reading experience.

Figure 34. Finding the benchmark levels

Looking More Closely at Benchmark Text Reading

Now that you have determined the three levels, you know the level to recommend for each child for independent reading and the level at which you will begin instruction. At this point, you will want to review the Benchmark Assessment results for additional information to inform instruction. We recommend looking carefully at the student's reading of at least one of the assessment conference texts. Choose the reading you feel provides the most information about the reader's text processing. Usually, this reading will be the Benchmark Instructional-level text. As you analyze the reading of the text, you can note the reading behaviors that the student controls, partially controls, or does not yet control. You can also examine the reader's ability to use the sources of information in the text.

Analyzing Sources of Information

To inform teaching, analyze the student's errors and self-corrections on her Benchmark Instructional-level text to find out what kinds of information the reader is using and what kinds of information are being neglected. For example, a reader who consistently makes substitution errors like *dog* for *puppy* may be thinking about the meaning of the story but neglecting to check with the letters in the word. A reader who consistently makes errors like *car* for *can* may be noticing the letters but neglecting to think about whether the reading sounds right and makes sense. (The *Professional Development* DVD provides support in decision making based on this information.)

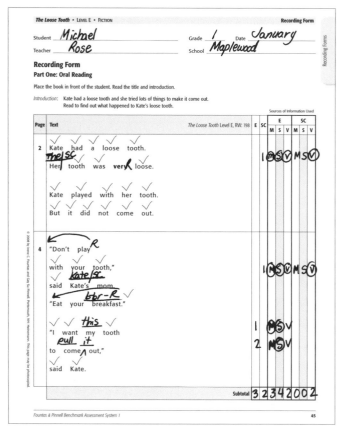

Figure 35. Coded oral reading of *The Loose Tooth*

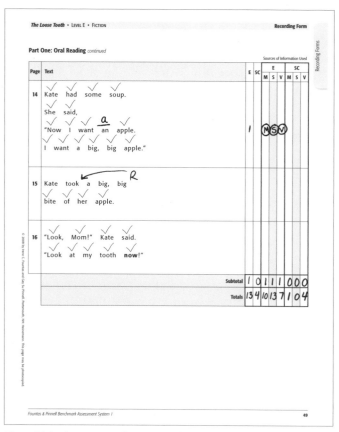

Figure 36. Analyzing errors for sources of information

After tallying each error and self-correction on the Recording Form, look at the number and kinds of errors and self-corrections the student has made. Look at the far right sources of information columns. Begin by writing *MSV* next to each error in the error column. For self-corrections, write *MSV* in the error column and in the self-correction column. For both the errors (E) and the self-corrections (SC), you are going to hypothesize and record the sources of information that the reader was using when he made the error or self-correction, determining if the child was using meaning (M), language structure (S), or visual information (V) at the time (see Figures 35 and 36). Alternatively, you can place a check (✓) in the column instead of writing *M, S, V.*

▶ *Meaning.* Readers often make substitutions that indicate they are thinking about the meaning of the text. For example, a reader might say *ballet* for *dance.* Ask yourself: Did the meaning of the text influence the error? If so, circle the *M* in the sources of information column under error (E).

▶ *Structure.* A powerful source of information for a reader is the structure of language. From our knowledge of oral language, we have implicit knowledge of the way words are put together to form phrases and sentences. It "sounds right" to us. Readers often substitute nouns for nouns or verbs for verbs, indicating an awareness of the structure of language. For example, a reader might say *We like going* for *We like to ride.* Ask yourself: Does the error fit an acceptable English language structure? Did structure influence the error? If so, circle the *S* in the sources of information column under error (E).

Note: Readers often use multiple sources of information as they process texts. You might code this as both *S* (the child substituted one verb construction for another) and *M* (*going* and *ride* both mean ways to get somewhere).

In another example, a reader might substitute *steps* for *stairs,* indicating attention to all three—meaning, language structure, and visual information. Here, you would circle *M, S,* and *V* in the sources of information column.

▶ *Visual information.* Readers use the visual features of print—the letters and words—to read. They connect these features to phonetic information that exists in their heads. For example, looking at the picture, a reader might say *park* for *play.* Ask yourself: Did the visual information from the print influence the error (letter, part, word)? If so, circle *V* in the error column.

Use a similar procedure for coding the reader's self-corrections. Here, you are hypothesizing the additional information that the reader might have used to correct the error. The self-correction, of course, indicates use of all three sources of information—meaning, language structure, and visual information—because it is the accurate word. But you are searching here for what the reader might have used as additional information to correct the error.

If the reader made the error *ballet* for *dance,* for example, and then self-corrected, the error would be analyzed as *M,* and in the self-correction column you would circle *S* and *V,* because the reader might have thought about the way the language sounded and might have noticed the *d.* If the reader said *park* for *play* and then self-corrected, you would circle *M* and *S* in the self-correction column, because the English language structure and the meaning of the text likely influenced the correction.

These analyses will help you look qualitatively at the reader's use of these different sources of information. Think about what the reader is neglecting. You can help the reader attend to the information sources needed as you listen to him read orally during reading lessons or do some teaching after the reading. If readers in a group are neglecting to think about what might make sense, you can prompt them to do so. If they are not noticing the first letter or another part of a word that would be helpful, you can draw it to their attention.

Noting Strategic Actions

Look again at the errors you have marked on the text in the Recording Form for the reader's Benchmark Instructional-level book. Think about the reader as a problem solver. Six areas will be helpful in your thinking:

▶ *Behaviors indicating attention to print features.* You want to look for evidence that the beginning reader knows how print "works," for example, matching one spoken word to one written word. If the reader does not show evidence of having these behaviors under control, you can do some explicit teaching.

▶ *Detecting errors.* Rather than reading along and ignoring errors, you want the reader to notice when something doesn't fit. Effective readers are constantly monitoring their own reading accuracy. If the reader does not show signs of checking on himself or self-monitoring, you can draw attention to mismatches and show him how to fix them.

▶ *Self-correcting.* Self-correction is a sign that the reader is monitoring his reading and working actively to make everything fit—meaning, structure, visual information, and the way the reading sounds. You can prompt for self-correction.

▶ *Searching for and using information.* Effective readers *actively* search for the information they need to read with accuracy, fluency, and understanding. They make attempts that, even if not right, show you they are trying out what they know. You can teach the reader many ways to search for and use multiple sources of information in the text.

▶ *Solving words.* You want readers to have and use many ways to solve words. As they

learn more, they will recognize many words automatically, but they also need to be able to use phonics and word analysis strategies so that they can learn many more. Then you can teach the reader many different ways to solve words.

▶ *Maintaining fluency.* Effective readers put all sources of information together so that their reading sounds fluent and expressive. They read in word groups and stop at punctuation; they stress words in bold and italic type. You can think about how the reading sounded. If the reader is not fluent and the text is easy enough, you can demonstrate fluent reading and show the reader how to put words together so that it sounds good, reading with intonation and logical word groupings.

The questions on pages 55 and 56 (Figure 37) will be helpful in guiding your thinking as you look at your coding and think about the reading behaviors you observed. The first section applies to the earliest levels (A and B). The other categories apply to all levels.

This guide can be copied or printed from the *Assessment Forms* book or CD-ROM for easy reference. The questions will help you focus on the actions the reader takes and will give you insight into how the reader uses different kinds of information and problem solves his way through the text. You will be able to notice effective and ineffective processing and listen for the reader's ability to maintain fluency. By using the guide regularly, you can train yourself to look beyond the numbers to the reading behaviors that will provide critical information for your teaching.

In the sample that follows (Figure 37), notice how one teacher has used the guide to note important behaviors that Enrico evidenced in his reading of *The Loose Tooth*. The teacher carefully considered the strategic actions Enrico controlled, partially controlled, or did not yet control. These notes inform her teaching.

Name: *Enrico*   Date: _____

Guide for Observing and Noting Reading Behaviors	Notes
1. Attention to Print Features *Does the reader:* • Move left to right across a line of print? • Return to the left for a new line? • Match word by word while reading a line or more of print? • Recognize a few easy high frequency words?	All early behaviors are well under control.
2. Detecting Errors *Does the reader:* • Hesitate at an unknown word? • Stop at an unknown word? • Stop at an unknown word and appeal for help? • Stop after an error? • Notice mismatches? • Notice when an attempt does not look right? • Notice when an attempt does not sound right? • Notice when an attempt does not make sense? • Reread to confirm reading? • Use knowledge of some high frequency words to check on reading? • Check one source of information with another? • Check an attempt that makes sense with language? • Check an attempt that makes sense with the letters (visual information)? • Use language structure to check on reading? • Request help after making several attempts?	Stops at unfamiliar words; usually tries first letter. Notices most errors. Repeats to confirm and search for information. Knows many high-frequency words. Checks meaning and structure with visual information.
3. Self-Correcting *Does the reader:* • Reread and try again until accurate? • Stop after an error and make another attempt? • Stop after an error and make multiple attempts until accurate? • Reread to self-correct? • Work actively to solve mismatches? • Self-correct errors some of the time? • Self-correct errors most of the time?	Does not usually make a second attempt. SC at point of error, does not reread. 1:4 errors
4. Searching for and Using Information **Meaning** *Does the reader:* • Make meaningful attempts at unknown words? • Use the meaning of the story or text to predict unknown words? • Reread to gather more information to solve a word? • Reread and use the meaning of the sentence? • Reread to search for more details—information, characters, plot? • Reread to gather information to clarify confusions? • Use headings and titles to think about the meaning of a section of text? • Use information in the pictures to help in understanding a text? • Use knowledge of the genre (and its characteristics) to help in understanding a text? • Use knowledge of the genre (and its characteristics) to help in finding information? • Use readers' tools to help in finding information (glossary, index)? **Structure** *Does the reader:* • Use knowledge of oral language to solve unknown words? • Reread to see if a word "sounds right" in a sentence? • Reread to correct using language structure?	Some attempts not self-corrected as he reads on; does not notice mismatch with visual info. or meaning. Uses info. from the pictures. Rereads sometimes to solve words but not to correct mismatches with structure.

Figure 37. Guide for Observing and Noting Reading Behaviors

Guide for Observing . . . (cont.)	Notes
Visual Information *Does the reader:* • Use the visual information to solve words? • Use the sound of the first letter(s) to attempt or solve a word? • Use some, most, or all of the visual information to solve words? • Use sound analysis to solve a word? • Make attempts that are visually similar? • Use knowledge of a high frequency word to problem solve? • Search for more visual information within a word to solve it? • Use analogy to solve unknown words? • Use syllables to solve words? • Use prefixes and suffixes to take apart and recognize words? • Use inflectional endings to problem solve words? • Recognize most words quickly and easily? • Reread and use the sound of the first letter to solve a word? • Problem solve unknown words quickly and efficiently? • Work actively to solve words? • Use two or three sources of information together in attempts at words? • Use all sources of information flexibly to solve words? • Use all sources of information in an orchestrated way?	*Uses first letters of words along with meaning and structure.* *Makes some attempts that are not visually similar.* *Rereads and uses the first letter to solve words.* *Some errors indicate using all sources of information.*
5. Solving Words *Does the reader:* • Recognize a core of high frequency words quickly? • Recognize most words quickly and easily? • Use a variety of flexible ways to take words apart? • Use the meaning of the sentences to solve words? • Use the structure of the sentence to solve words? • Use some of the visual information to solve words? • Use known word parts to solve words? • Use sound analysis (sounding out)? • Use analogy to solve words? • Make attempts that are visually similar? • Use the sound of the first letter to solve words? • Work actively to solve words? • Use known words or parts to solve unknown words? • Use syllables to problem solve? • Use prefixes and suffixes to take words apart? • Use inflectional endings to take words apart? • Use sentence context to derive the meaning of words? • Use base words and root words to derive the meaning of words? • Make connections among words to understand their meaning?	*Recognizes most words up to level E.* *Shows evidence of rapid word recognition on words he knows.* *Uses the first letter but seldom goes beyond it.*
6. Maintaining Fluency *Does the reader:* • Read without pointing? • Read word groups (phrases)? • Put words together? • Read smoothly? • Read the punctuation? • Make the voice go down at periods? • Make the voice go up at question marks? • Pause briefly at commas, dashes, and hyphens? • Read dialogue with intonation or expression? • Stress the appropriate words to convey accurate meaning? • Read at a good rate—not too fast and not too slow?	*Reads some words in phrases. Does not need to point at this level. Notices and pauses at commas and ending marks.*
7. Other	

Resources

Figure 37. Guide for observing and noting reading behaviors

Using your notes on the Guide for Observing and Noting Reading Behaviors, make notes on your Assessment Summary form in the boxes labeled "additional comments" and "instructional implications" (see Figure 38). Your observations of the processing or problem-solving actions the reader is able to use will have important implications for the instruction you provide in your lessons.

Once you have completed an Assessment Summary, you can enter the data into the *Data Management* CD-ROM. Doing so will allow you to track progress over time, analyze trends in reading performance, and compare data within your class in order to inform instructional plans. After you review and analyze the scores and the strategic actions, note your thinking about areas of the reading process that have important instructional implications. See the following section, "Connecting Benchmark Assessment Results to Instruction," for a summary of ways the assessment can inform instruction.

Expanding Performance Evidence or Diagnosis with Optional Assessments

The extensive information gathered through the basic Benchmark Assessment procedures outlined above provides clear direction for instruction, but you may also wish to get more diagnostic evidence about the student's literacy knowledge through the optional assessments in the *Assessment Forms* book and CD-ROM (Appendix B). A Reading Interview, an array of Phonics and Word Analysis Assessments, and a variety of Vocabulary Assessments will provide targeted information about the learner's knowledge in specific areas of literacy learning.

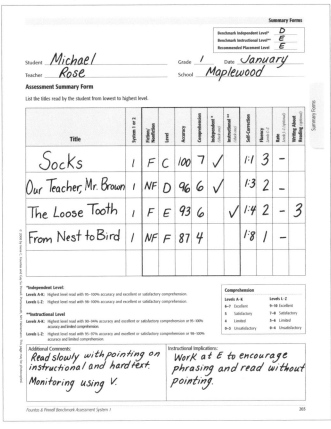

Figure 38. Michael's Assessment Summary

Connecting Benchmark Assessment
Results to Instruction

In our view, the most important use of assessment is to inform instruction. Even while administering and analyzing the benchmark conference, you will find yourself thinking about what the student needs in terms of instruction. When you have completed the assessment, you will have valuable categories of information that will allow you to link your findings directly with instruction.

In this section, we discuss and provide models for using assessment results to place students in groups; to plan for individual, small-group, and whole-class instruction; and to use *The Continuum of Literacy Learning* to connect assessment and instruction.

Grouping Children for Instruction

The three levels (Benchmark Independent, Benchmark Instructional, and Recommended Placement) you determined will help you form groups for reading instruction (see Figures 39 and 40). List your students on the Class Record form from lowest to highest placement level to help you cluster students appropriately. The *Data Management* CD-ROM will allow you to sort a class roster by benchmark level (or other variable), which can assist with instructional groupings.

With the wide range of students in every classroom, it is a challenge to form reading groups that will work efficiently. Ideally, you would have a group for each level, but for the class below, that would mean too many groups. It would take so much time to teach the groups that students would not get reading instruction often enough. Also, there are slight differences in children's processing systems even if they are reading at about the same text level.

Mrs. Belini used all the data to make her grouping decisions. Sometimes she clustered students who were at slightly different levels together in the same group. On the Class Record form, you can see that Devlin's instructional level is D, but the teacher placed him at C because his independent reading level is only B, his fluency at D was not good, and though he was accurate, he worked very slowly and hard to solve unknown words. Spencer's reading level is well above grade level. Mrs. Belini decided to teach him in a group with children reading at level I to give him group opportunities, however, and will challenge him in other ways through independent reading and writing about reading. In Figure 40, you can see the four reading groups she formed and her comments about teaching levels.

Benchmark assessment and ongoing assessment allow you to group dynamically as students develop differently from each other. Dynamic grouping means that you move children from group to group as they progress at different rates. You will adjust your groupings as needed. Small, homogeneous groups will enable you to choose appropriate texts and teach closely to the needs of the individual students.

Figure 39. Class benchmark levels

Sample Grouping for Mrs. Belini's Grade 1 Class				
Group	Carmen Demetrius David Shawn Pam	Devlin Ben Jerry Shelly Chaundra Joel	Jerome Sherry Conde Janelle Paul Christy	Steve Katia Stacy Anna Spencer
Comments	Need strong support to develop the early reading behaviors and acquire known words.	Provide extra challenge to Shelly, Chaundra, and Joel.	Provide extra challenge to Janelle, Paul, and Christy.	Give more support to Steve. Provide extra reading for Spencer.
Starting level	Start at B	Start at C	Start at E	Start at I; move quickly to J

Figure 40. Grouping for reading

We do not recommend naming the groups so they have permanent group status. Just call the group by the children's names or by the book they read last and invite them to come to the reading table. Also, you will want to have children work in other kinds of groups (for example, literacy work groups or heterogeneous literature discussion groups) that are not arranged by reading level. In addition to targeted small-group reading instruction, they will need many other group opportunities for age- and grade-appropriate instruction in interactive read-aloud or shared reading contexts.

Individual Instruction	
Data from Benchmark Assessment	**How the Information Helps in Making Teaching Decisions in Literacy Contexts**
▶ Benchmark Independent level ▶ Benchmark Instructional level ▶ Recommended Placement level	▶ Guiding students' book choices for independent reading ▶ Placing the student in a small group for instruction ▶ Reconsidering grouping decisions regarding the individual ▶ Informing individual reading conferences
▶ Evidence of processing (strategic actions and MSV analysis)	▶ Interacting with individuals in guided reading lessons ▶ Interacting with individuals in conferences
▶ Fluency score	▶ Interacting with individuals in guided reading or small-group lessons ▶ Interacting in individual conferences during reading workshop
▶ Comprehension category scores and total score	▶ Interacting with individuals during guided reading or small-group lessons ▶ Interacting with individuals in reading conferences ▶ Responding to writing about reading in the reader's notebook

Figure 41. Benchmark scores and teaching decisions for individuals

Planning Individual, Small-Group, and Whole-Class Instruction

Now let's think about how to use the rich information you collected as you begin working with your students in three instructional contexts: the teaching you do with individuals, small groups, and your entire class (see Figures 41–43).

Individual Instruction

The independent level will help you to put together browsing boxes or to guide the students' book choices for productive indepen-

dent reading. The Benchmark Assessment data are the foundation for placing students in "just right" books for small-group instruction. These levels will also help you think about forming groups of students who, while they are individuals and unique in many ways, are alike enough to teach together effectively. Students learn to read better by reading many texts each day. Easy reading has many benefits.

You can gather evidence of processing through analyzing the errors and self-correction behaviors of the student. Use this information to help you as you interact with the student individually during guided reading and read-

Small-Group Instruction	
Data from Benchmark Assessment	**How the Information Helps in Making Teaching Decisions in Literacy Contexts**
▷ Benchmark Independent level ▷ Benchmark Instructional level ▷ Recommended Placement level	▷ Making decisions about grouping ▷ Selecting texts for guided reading or small-group lessons
▷ Evidence of processing (strategic actions and MSV analysis)	▷ Preparing an introduction to the text for a guided reading lesson ▷ Making teaching points in guided reading lessons ▷ Planning word work for the end of the guided reading lesson
▷ Fluency scores	▷ Selecting texts for guided reading or small-group lessons ▷ Making teaching points in guided reading lessons ▷ Selecting ways to reread the text (readers' theater, shared reading)
▷ Comprehension category scores and total score	▷ Introducing texts to students in guided reading lessons ▷ Supporting the student's reading of the text ▷ Discussing the meaning of the text after reading ▷ Making teaching points in guided reading lessons ▷ Extending meaning of a text through writing about reading

Figure 42. Benchmark scores and teaching decisions for small groups

ing conferences. It will also help you to make teaching points in guided reading lessons.

The fluency score and your observation of oral reading will help you know what the student needs in terms of fluency support. It can inform your interactions with the student during guided reading and individual reading conferences. The comprehension category will help you know whether you need to intervene to help the student think more actively before, during, and after reading. Looking at the student's responses in categories (within, beyond, and about texts) will inform your interactions with the student during guided reading and individual conferences.

Small-Group Instruction

The Benchmark Instructional and Recommended Placement levels of your class will help you to form groups and select texts for them to read. Examining the demands of texts at that level will be helpful in constructing introductions to texts before students read them. You can look at the evidence of processing (see Figure 37, Guide for Observing and Noting Reading Behaviors) for each student, searching for patterns across the group. Chances are, there will be similar needs. Use this information to inform your teaching points after reading.

Whole-Class Instruction	
Data from Benchmark Assessment	**How the Information Helps in Making Teaching Decisions in Literacy Contexts**
▶ Benchmark Independent levels ▶ Benchmark Instructional levels	▶ Stocking the classroom library with books for self-selected independent reading ▶ Giving book talks to students in reading workshop ▶ Providing audio-recorded books for rereading and for literature discussion
▶ Evidence of processing (strategic actions and MSV analysis)	▶ Designing minilessons for reading workshop (strategies and skills) ▶ Engaging students in intentional conversation in interactive read-aloud ▶ Planning word study minilessons ▶ Engaging students in literature discussion
▶ Fluency scores	▶ Engaging students in shared and performance reading ▶ Providing effective models of oral reading through interactive read-aloud
▶ Comprehension category scores and total score	▶ Engaging students in intentional conversation during interactive read-aloud ▶ Engaging students in literature discussion ▶ Providing minilessons (strategies and skills; craft)

Figure 43. Benchmark scores and teaching decisions for whole classes

The fluency scores of individuals in the group help you decide whether to do some intensive teaching or prompt for fluency and phrasing as students read the text. You may want to incorporate readers' theater into your small-group work to help them be more conscious of how their reading sounds.

The comprehension scores will help you know how much you need to support students' active thinking. Of course, you will always be teaching for comprehending because that is one of the main goals of instruction. But you may find that you need to adjust the text level to one that is very accessible and work intensively to get students to express their thinking. Looking at the patterns of performance within categories will help you plan teaching points and design activities for writing about reading that will also extend students' thinking about texts.

Whole-Class Instruction

Individual assessment can inform your teaching of the whole class as well. Use your class list to look at the classroom library. Make sure that you have a quantity of high-quality books at levels your students can read independently. Also, as you make book talks to students, present a range of levels. It is extremely important for students to process a large quantity of text independently every day. You are helping them take on more difficult texts through guided reading instruction, but they also need to be building stamina and skill on their own.

Look across the assessment data for information on processing and comprehension. It's especially important to look at the extent to which students can express their thinking beyond and about texts. This information will be invaluable as you plan minilessons for reading workshop and for intentional conversation during interactive read-aloud. We use the term *intentional conversation* to remind ourselves that we need to simultaneously engage in a real conversation with students and have in mind things that we want to teach them during read-aloud sessions. (See *Teaching for Comprehending and Fluency* [Heinemann, 2006], chapters 15–17, for more description.) Finally, you can use the information to help extend students' thinking through writing about reading as part of interactive read-aloud and literature discussion.

Connecting Assessment to Instruction with *The Continuum of Literacy Learning*

As you think about individual, small-group, and whole-class instruction, you will find it helpful to consult *The Continuum of Literacy Learning (K–2): A Guide to Teaching* (Fountas and Pinnell, in press, Heinemann). This volume contains seven continua (see Figure 44 on page 66). Each continuum focuses on an area of the language arts curriculum. Six continua—Interactive Read-Aloud and Literature Discussion; Shared and Performance Reading; Writing About Reading; Writing; Oral, Visual, and Technological Communication; and Phonics, Spelling, and Word Study—provide grade-level expectations and are designed for planning group instruction. The seventh, the Guided Reading continuum, is organized by Fountas and Pinnell levels from A–N and correlates directly with the benchmark levels you arrived at through the Benchmark Assessment. Once you have determined a child's benchmark and placement levels, turn directly to the Guided Reading continuum and find the direct link from the Fountas & Pinnell Benchmark Assessment System to instruction.

The continua provide specific descriptions of the texts that students read, listen to, write, and perform. In addition, each continuum lists specific behaviors and understandings that are required at each level for students to demonstrate thinking *within*, *beyond*, and *about* the text. Taken together, these behaviors and understandings represent the demands of the text. They form what students will be expected to do in order to effectively read and understand the text. The behaviors and understandings are accumulative across the levels. In other words, the reader is taking on new demands as the texts grow more challenging. A student reading level M and successfully meeting the demands of the text is also able to meet the demands of texts on levels A–L.

The Continuum of Literacy Learning, K–2	
Continuum	**Description**
Guided Reading Levels A–N	The teacher works with a small group of children who are similar in their development of a reading process. The teacher introduces the text and the students read it with teaching support.
Interactive Read-Aloud and Literature Discussion Grades K–2	The teacher reads aloud to students and engages them in intentional conversation. Students discuss their thinking in the whole group or in small groups. This continuum also refers to "book clubs," in which students independently read (or listen to) books and then discuss them in small groups.
Shared and Performance Reading Grades K–2	Students read together (or in parts) a text that they know well. They show with their voices what the text means.
Writing About Reading Grades K–2	Students respond to reading by writing and sometimes drawing.
Writing Grades K–2	Students engage in the writing process and produce pieces of their own writing in many genres.
Oral, Visual, and Technological Communication Grades K–2	Oral language is used across the curriculum and is embedded in all contexts in all continua. In this continuum, specific expectations are listed and extended to interactive media.
Phonics, Spelling, and Word Study Grades K–2	This continuum includes expectations related to nine areas of learning: early literacy concepts, phonological awareness, letter knowledge, letter-sound relationships, spelling patterns, high-frequency words, word meaning/vocabulary, word structure, and word-solving actions.

Figure 44. The Continuum of Literacy Learning, K–2

Working Step by Step with Benchmark Assessment and the Continuum

Next we provide step-by-step examples for connecting benchmark assessments to guided reading, interactive read-aloud, and whole-group reading minilessons in a reading workshop.

Linking Information to Guided Reading Lessons

Step 1. Assess all students in the class and find Benchmark Independent, Benchmark Instructional, and Recommended Placement levels.

Step 2. Form temporary groups according to their placement levels.

Step 3. Go to the Guided Reading continuum and look at the characteristics of the texts at the level. Keep these characteristics in mind when selecting books for the group.

Step 4. Select several possible books for each group so that you will have alternatives across a few days or a week of instruction.

Step 5. Select the text that you will introduce to the group first.

Step 6. Read the text carefully with the characteristics in mind.

Step 7. Look at your student data on strategic actions and sources of information as well as fluency and comprehension. Think about what students need to learn how to do as readers. Reports from the *Data Management* CD-ROM can be helpful in identifying and analyzing patterns.

Step 8. Look at the behaviors and understandings for the level. These represent what students need to be able to do to read successfully at the level.

Step 9. Think about what your students can do and then find behaviors and understandings that they partially control or do not yet control.

Step 10. Plan your introduction to the text and teaching points for the lesson, keeping in mind the processing needs of your students.

Step 11. Plan for word work at the end of the lesson. You will find specific suggestions for each level on the continuum, A–N.

Step 12. Plan for writing about reading (optional element). Here, think about the specific demands of text on the Guided Reading continuum. Then, look at the Writing About Reading continuum for the grade level. Look at the genres that are appropriate and the thinking that students are expected to do.

Step 13. As students grow more proficient and reading becomes easy at the level, look at the behaviors and understandings for the next highest level. You'll find many of the same strategies for which you've been teaching, because the reading process is built by applying the same set of complex strategies to increasingly more difficult texts. You may find new understandings or more complex versions of the same understandings. Start to look toward this next level.

Step 14. Select texts from the next level and look at the text characteristics and behaviors and understandings to notice, teach, and support.

Step 15. Continue to introduce texts and teach lessons based on the spiraling of text demands.

Linking Assessment Information to Teaching in Interactive Read-Aloud

Step 1. Assess the class and find Benchmark Independent, Benchmark Instructional, and Recommended Placement levels.

Step 2. Look at the total scores for comprehension and scores within each category (within, beyond, and about the text). Reports from the *Data Management* CD-ROM can be helpful in identifying and analyzing patterns.

Step 3. Look for patterns across the entire group. Even though students are reading at different levels, there may be some similar needs in terms of comprehending and processing.

Step 4. Go to the Interactive Read-Aloud continuum for the grade level.

Step 5. Look at the characteristics of texts and keep them in mind as you select books to read aloud to students.

Step 6. Select and sequence texts so that students will make connections between them and build on previous understandings.

Step 7. Look at the behaviors and understandings and think about your students' needs in terms of active thinking within, beyond, and about texts.

Step 8. Select goals to accomplish in your interactive read-aloud program.

Step 9. Plan an "opening" to each text that will help your students think more deeply about the text or notice important information and characteristics. The opening should be brief, just a few words to set readers up for successful understanding (see Chapter 15, *Teaching for Comprehending and Fluency, K–8*).

Step 10. Plan intentional conversation and "turn and talk" routines (see Chapter 18, *Teaching for Comprehending and Fluency, K–8*) to support your students' thinking as you think and talk through the text together.

Step 11. Plan for writing about reading (optional element). Here, think about the specific demands of the texts on the Interactive Read-Aloud continuum. Then, look at the Writing About Reading continuum for the grade level. Look at the genres that are appropriate and the thinking that students are expected to do.

Step 12. Keep a class record of books read aloud so that you and the students can easily remember connections and make new ones.

Linking Assessment Information to Whole-Group Minilessons in a Reading Workshop

Step 1. Assess the class and find Benchmark Independent, Benchmark Instructional, and Recommended Placement levels.

Step 2. Look at the total scores on comprehension and scores within each category (within, beyond, and about the text).

Step 3. Look at the evidence of processing—strategic actions and analysis of sources of information (MSV).

Step 4. Look for patterns across the entire group. Even though students are reading at different levels, there may be some similar needs in terms of comprehending and processing.

Step 5. Go to the Interactive Read-Aloud continuum. Look at the behaviors and understandings to notice, teach, and support.

Step 6. Think about your students' needs in terms of active thinking within, beyond, and about texts.

Step 7. Select goals and understandings that lend themselves to effective teaching in minilessons.

Step 8. Plan a minilesson (or short series of lessons) to address the goals.

Step 9. Plan for writing about reading (optional element). Here, think about the specific demands of the texts on the Interactive Read-Aloud continuum. Then, look at the Writing About Reading continuum for the grade level. Look at the genres that are appropriate and the thinking that students are expected to do.

Step 10. Students write about reading during their independent work time. They write about the books they have chosen for independent reading.

Step 11. Use the list of behaviors and understandings to guide them in their writing.

Step 12. In grade 2 and up, you may be using a reader's notebook for various forms of writing including dialogue letters. Prompt and look for evidence of behaviors and understandings in students' writing. (See *Teaching for Comprehending and Fluency* for specific lessons on using a reader's notebook.)

Connecting the Assessment to a Core or Basal Reading Program

The correlation between information gained from Benchmark Assessments and a leveled book reading program is clear. Identification of the Benchmark Independent and Instructional levels will allow you to guide the selection of independent reading books and choose books for instruction that are at the optimal level for supporting young readers. You can read detailed descriptions of the levels with sample texts in *Leveled Books K–8: Matching Texts to Readers for Effective Teaching* (Heinemann, 2006) and find over 20,000 leveled book titles in *The Fountas and Pinnell Leveled Book List, K–8* (Heinemann, 2006) and at fountasand-pinnellleveledbooks.com.

Benchmark Assessment results can inform more than leveled reading programs. You may be using, for reading instruction, a set of materials that is usually referred to as a "basal" or "core" system. Most systems consist of anthologies of written material. The anthology may include stories written especially for reading instruction or drawn from various works of literature. Selections are sequenced in the anthologies.

With a core or basal system, you still need to think about readability. Understanding the demands of the texts will help you support and teach your students more effectively. Many core programs involve students in small-group reading instruction in addition to whole-group reading in the core anthology. The whole-group reading is usually in the form of read-aloud or shared reading. The basal system ideally includes sets of leveled books to differentiate instruction. Figure 45 will help you make the connection between the Fountas and Pinnell Benchmark Instructional level and the basal system if you are using the anthology stories for small-group teaching. Use the benchmark books and their characteristics to help you "level" the materials in your basal system.

Level Correspondence—Core or Basal Reading Programs

Fountas and Pinnell Benchmark Instructional Level	Guided Reading Level (for instruction)	Basal System Level
A	A	Kindergarten
B	B	Kindergarten
C	C	Preprimer
D	D	Preprimer
E	E	Preprimer
F	F	Primer
G	G	Primer
H	H	Grade 1 (middle)
I	I	Grade 1 (late)
J	J	Grade 2 (early)
K	K	Grade 2 (early)
L	L	Grade 2 (late)
M	M	Grade 2 (late)
N	N	Grade 3 (early)
O	O	Grade 3 (early)
P	P	Grade 3 (late)
Q	Q	Grade 4 (early)
R	R	Grade 4 (early)
S	S	Grade 4 (late)
T	T	Grade 5 (early)
U	U	Grade 5 (early)
V	V	Grade 5 (late)
W	W	Grade 6 (early)
X	X	Grade 6 (early)
Y	Y	Grade 6 (late)
Z	Z	Grades 7 and 8

Figure 45. Benchmark levels correlated to guided reading and core textbook levels

Case Studies: Interpreting and Using Benchmark Assessment Data

The interpretation and use of Benchmark Assessment data are more important than the scores themselves. In this section, we present four examples of readers, along with our interpretations and teacher commentary.

Jared, Grade 1 Student

In the figures below, you see Jared's Where-to-Start Word Test (Figure 46); his Recording Forms, with fluency ratings, for levels A, B, and C (Figures 47, 48, 49); his Assessment Summary (Figure 50); his Early Literacy Behaviors Assessment (Figure 51), and his Letter Recognition sheet (Figure 52).

Jared scored 11 on the Where-to-Start Word Test. The results showed that he could read simple high-frequency words such as *I, to, my, we, in, like, it, Mom, is, see,* and *at*. These easy

words appear often in level A and B storybooks. Recognizing them gives Jared a way to monitor his reading. These familiar words free him to notice other challenges in the text.

Oral Reading. Jared read three texts, *Best Friends* (level A) at 97% accuracy, *Playing* (level B) at 91%, and *Shopping* (level C) at 89%.

Across the three readings, it was apparent that Jared was using meaning and language structure to help him in reading. On level A, his substitution of *ballet* for *dance* did not fit the structure of the sentence. Probably he was thinking of "do ballet," indicating a connection with meaning. On the next error (*build* for *climb*), he might at first have been looking at the picture of children climbing on what looks like big blocks, but he then appeared to notice visual features of the word *climb*, check it with the picture, and come up with the accurate word. On one line of print, we can observe evidence that Jared was cross-checking visual information with meaning.

On the level B text, he again showed evidence that he can use both meaning and visual features of words. He handled this predictable text well, although his sense of language structure tended to override visual information on the first three pages (reading "I like playing" for "I like to play"). In fact, had he not made these errors, his accuracy rate would have been much higher. His substitution made sense and sounded right to him, and he neglected the visual information. On page 6, however, Jared did cross-check with visual information and, this time, self-corrected. The teacher observed that Jared sometimes ceased pointing to individual words and slid his finger along. He will need to continue to point until word-by-word matching is strongly established.

On the level C text, Jared read below 90% accuracy but showed considerable strength. Throughout his text, he was trying to make the reading make sense, although he did not seem to notice when his reading conflicted with the

continued on page 76

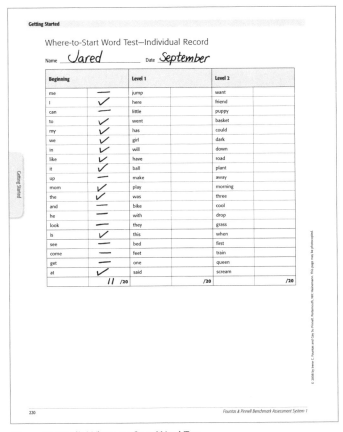

Figure 46. Jared's Where-to-Start Word Test

Level A — Benchmark Independent

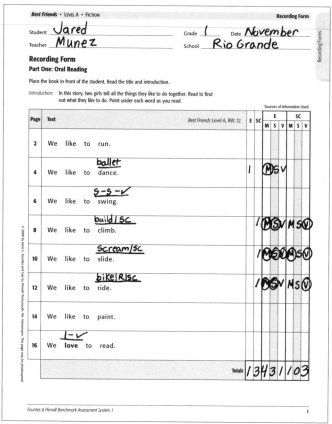

Figure 47a. Jared's Recording Form, level A

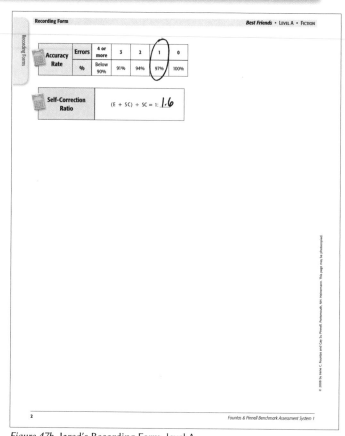

Figure 47b. Jared's Recording Form, level A

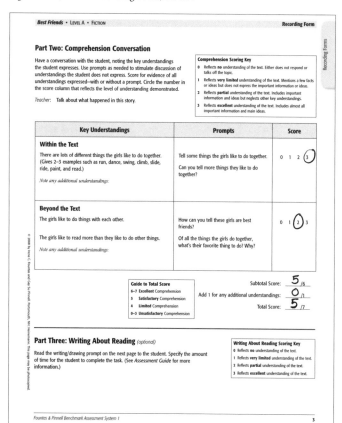

Figure 47c. Jared's Recording Form, level A

Level B — Benchmark Instructional

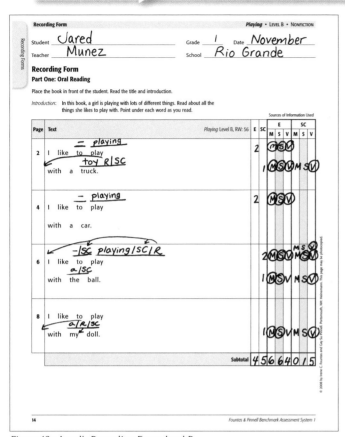

Figure 48a. Jared's Recording Form, level B

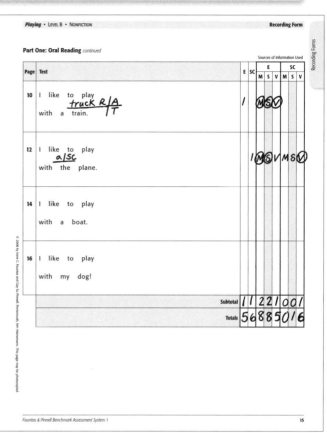

Figure 48b. Jared's Recording Form, level B

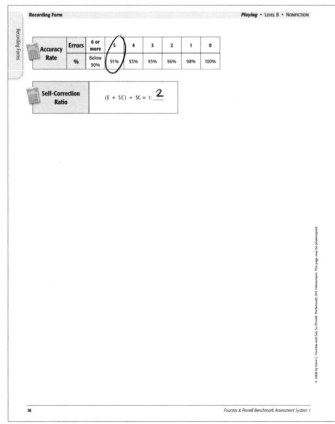

Figure 48c. Jared's Recording Form, level B

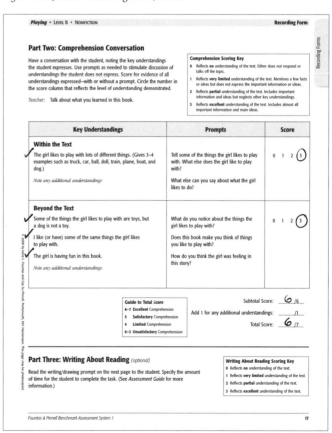

Figure 48d. Jared's Recording Form, level B

Level C — Hard Text

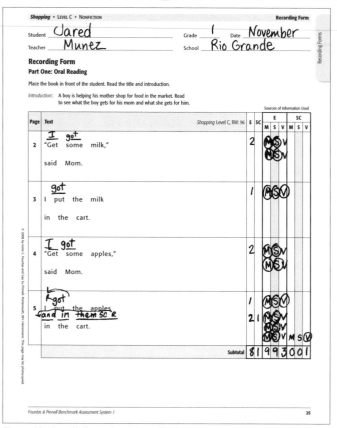

Figure 49a. Jared's Recording Form, level C

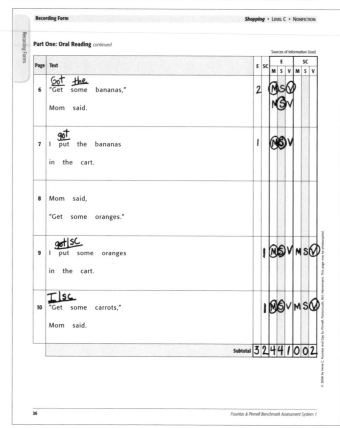

Figure 49b. Jared's Recording Form, level C

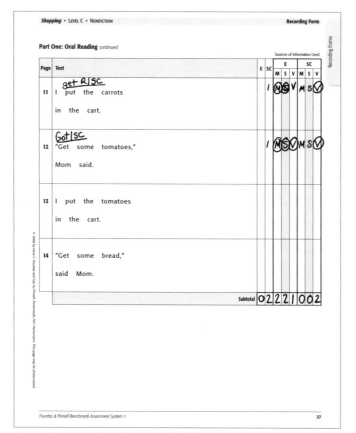

Figure 49c. Jared's Recording Form, level C

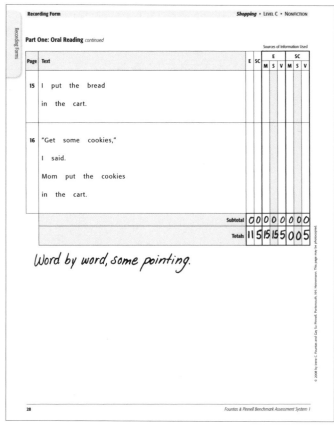

Figure 49d. Jared's Recording Form, level C

Level C — Hard Text (continued)

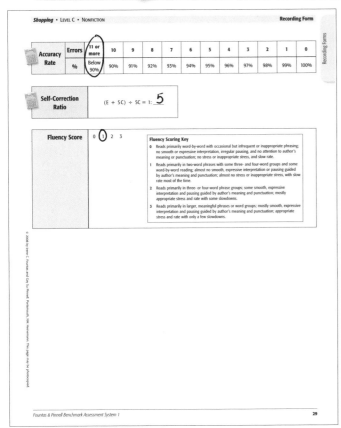

Figure 49e. Jared's Recording Form, level C

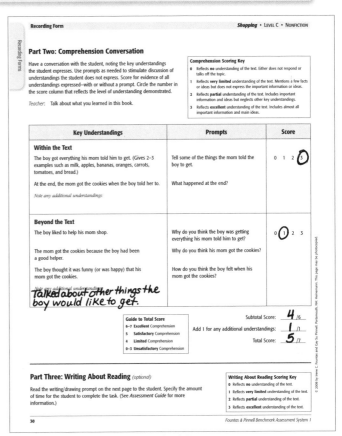

Figure 49f. Jared's Recording Form, level C

Figure 50. Jared's Assessment Summary

Figure 51. Jared's Early Literacy Behaviors assessment—individual record

overall meaning of the text. There was little self-correction; this behavior indicates that he is not noticing mismatches to monitor his reading. Later, after being corrected, he was able to read these same words accurately, indicating that he could remember them as meaningful units and use them again as cued by text.

Comprehension Conversation. Jared was able to talk about important details for all of the texts he read. He scored 5 or 6 on all levels. When discussing *Playing*, he was able to name some of the things the girl played with but also made connections to his own experiences. When discussing *Shopping*, he could name some of the good things that the boy put in the cart, but did not describe the general idea of the mom telling the child to "get things" and the boy doing it. He did not respond when asked why the mom got the cookies for the boy.

Letter Recognition and *Early Literacy Behaviors (optional assessments)*. To explore

early understandings (see Figure 51), the teacher began on level B, *My Little Dog*, and used the additional questions related to early literacy understandings. Jared's responses indicated that he understands a great deal about print. He knows that "first" in reading means at the top on the left margin, but he is still uncertain about "return sweep." He can locate letters and words that are embedded in print. He could locate an unknown word, *play*, in the text by saying it and using visual features. When asked to locate a word that starts with a particular letter, however, he simply pointed to another letter within a word. The assessment provided evidence that Jared has good beginning knowledge of letters both in isolation and within words.

Jared is still working to gain control of early reading behaviors. Jared recognized and called by name forty-eight of fifty-two characters (upper- and lowercase letters) on the Letter Recognition Assessment (Figure 52). He could match word by word on one line of print but was unable to sustain this behavior across the second line, indicating that he is beginning to control directionality and word-by-word matching but that he needs further teaching in these areas.

Jared's teacher, Ms. Munez, shared her thinking about Jared following her assessment. Figure 53 is a transcript of her oral commentary.

Figure 52. Jared's Letter Recognition

Ms. Munez Talks About Jared

Analysis of Assessment. I learned a lot about Jared from this assessment. Looking across everything, I would place him at level B.

He has good letter knowledge and can also recognize letters when they are part of words. He also knows a few high-frequency words that he can use as signposts. I was impressed with his understanding of the level C book *Shopping*. However, he was under 90% accuracy; he might be able to read level C with my help, but several things concern me.

As he began reading the text, he read "'I got some milk,' said Mom." That reading makes sense only superficially. Mom was actually telling the child to get the milk. I don't expect Jared to notice the middle vowel that distinguishes *get* from *got*, but I would expect him to cross-check *I* and *got*, since he knows the word *I* and also knows the most common sound of the letter *g*.

He gained momentum as he read through the text, reading the last part of it accurately. But he was able to achieve this accuracy because of three "tolds." On this harder text, Jared was not able to solve words effectively. Also, I have noted that his responses on "return sweep" were weak and he seemed to lose control of word-by-word matching when expected to process more than one line of text. Although I think he will move quickly to level C, I would like to use level B texts for a short time to firm up early reading behaviors.

The Continuum as a Resource. As I work with him on level B, I can take the opportunity to teach for word-by-word matching and return sweep, especially with texts that have more than two lines. I can also help him expand his knowledge of high-frequency words so that he has more signposts. Looking at the *Continuum of Literacy Learning*, I would select the following goals for teaching Jared in guided reading:

▷ achieve complete control of word-by-word matching and directionality

▷ use the first letter of a word in connection with language syntax to solve it

▷ continue to cross-check different kinds of information against each other to monitor and self-correct reading

▷ reread to search for and use information

▷ begin to notice ending punctuation

▷ make predictions using personal experiences and knowledge

▷ make connections between personal experiences and texts

▷ talk about details in the pictures and what they reveal about the problem or characters' feelings

▷ understand and discuss the ideas in a text

Figure 53. Ms. Munez's comments about Jared's reading

Continued on next page

Looking ahead to level C, I know that Jared will need to recognize more high frequency words and to begin to use known words to make connections and solve them. He will also need to be very active in monitoring his reading, using several sources of information to check on accuracy, and to process slightly longer, more complex sentences. He can prepare for level C by achieving automatic control of some early behaviors, such as matching, by increasing the number of known words and letter-sound cues, and by continuing to process sentences as language and to think about the meaning.

For word work in level B, I plan to have Jared and members of his reading group do the following:

- ▶ sort letters in a variety of ways

- ▶ find letters in an array and name them

- ▶ read simple high-frequency words on the white board

- ▶ make high-frequency words with magnetic letters

- ▶ make CVC (consonant, vowel, consonant) words and then change the first letter to make a new word (phonogram patterns)

- ▶ write a variety of CVC words quickly on a whiteboard

Figure 53. Ms. Munez's comments about Jared's reading *(continued)*

Wyatt, Grade 1 Student

In the figures on the following pages, you see Wyatt's Where-to-Start Word Test (Figure 54); his Recording Forms, with fluency ratings, for levels H, I, and J (Figures 55, 56, 57); and his Assessment Summary (Figure 58).

Wyatt scored a perfect 20 on the level 1 word list and read 18 words on the level 2 list. Additionally, he could read six words on the level 3 list.

Oral Reading. He read *Bubbles*, the level G nonfiction text, with very high accuracy. Then he read *The Sleepover Party*, level H, fiction, at 98%, with a fluency rating of 2. He read *The Best Cat*, level I, fiction, at 94% accuracy, with a fluency rating of 2, and then read *Our New Neighbors*, fiction, level J at 89% accuracy and a 1 on the fluency scoring key.

Wyatt's errors and self-corrections indicate that he was using visual features of words, looking beyond the first letter. For example:

▶ On *The Sleepover Party*, he made just five substitutions, among them: *ask/also, ready/really, father/favorite,* and *bag/backpack,* which was self-corrected.

▶ On *The Best Cat*, he made many more substitutions, seeming to rely on initial sounds.

▶ On *Our New Neighbors*, he made lots of substitutions, as shown on his Recording Form.

At the same time, even though he read with high accuracy and demonstrated good word solving, Wyatt often neglected to search for further information to make all sources fit. Sometimes his reading did not make sense, but Wyatt did not make further attempts. He read on, ignoring the error. For example:

▶ On *The Sleepover Party*, he substituted *ask* for *also* in the sentence: "But he was also a little worried." At another place in the text, he read "Jim wasn't ready listening" for "Jim wasn't really listening."

▶ On *The Best Cat*, Wyatt read *from* for *furry* in this sentence: "He wanted a cat that would sleep on his bed and purr in his ear and be his best furry friend." He substituted *from*, a known high-frequency word, for several words in the text, including *furry* and *farmer*. Each time, he lost meaning with this error.

▶ On *Our New Neighbors*, he substituted *house* for *horses*, both words that he might have been expected to know. In addition, this substitution obviously did not make sense in the sentence. He also substituted *until* for *enough*, indicating a loss of meaning as well as neglect of visual information.

Across all texts, Wyatt needed to read with greater fluency. On level H, he was able to read the text in mostly meaningful phrases and used some expression, but on the highest levels, he read slowly, word by word.

Comprehension Conversation. He was able to demonstrate strong understanding of *The Sleepover Party*, scoring a 3 on thinking within and beyond the text. He inferred that Jim's mom put the toy (Mugsy) in his backpack. He said, "He was worried and his mom knew that he'd be sad without Mugsy, so she put it in his bag when he wasn't looking. It was a surprise."

When discussing *The Best Cat*, he described the general plot of the text—that none of the cats liked the boy or wanted to be his cat. He demonstrated a grasp of the "twist" of the plot (that the cat chose the boy) and another main idea (that the best cat is the one who likes you). He did not make connections to his own pets or any other stories he has read about cats. On *The Best Cat*, the teacher scored Wyatt's discussion as: within the text = 3 and beyond the text = 3, additional understandings = 0.

Our New Neighbors was hard for Wyatt, although he scored close to 90% accuracy. He was able to recount that the new neighbors invited everyone to see their horses and said, "They kept it a big secret because they wanted it to be a surprise." He did not demonstrate the underlying idea that everyone was so surprised because they never thought the horses would be a carousel. He did connect the story to his own ride on a carousel.

Writing About Reading. In Figure 59, you see Wyatt's writing in response to *The Best Cat*, which he read at instructional level. In Figure 60, Wyatt's teacher, Mr. Gilbert, shares his thinking following the assessment.

Where-to-Start Word Test—Individual Record

Name Wyatt Date September

Beginning		Level 1		Level 2	
me		jump	✓	want	✓
I		here	✓	friend	✓
can		little	✓	puppy	✓
to		went	✓	basket	buckle
my		has	✓	could	✓
we		girl	✓	dark	✓
in		will	✓	down	✓
like		have	✓	road	✓
it		ball	✓	plant	✓
up		make	✓	away	✓
mom		play	✓	morning	✓
the		was	✓	three	✓
and		bike	✓	cool	cold
he		with	✓	drop	✓
look		they	✓	grass	✓
is		this	✓	when	✓
see		bed	✓	first	✓
come		feet	✓	train	✓
get		one	✓	queen	✓
at		said	✓	scream	✓
	/20		20/20		18/20

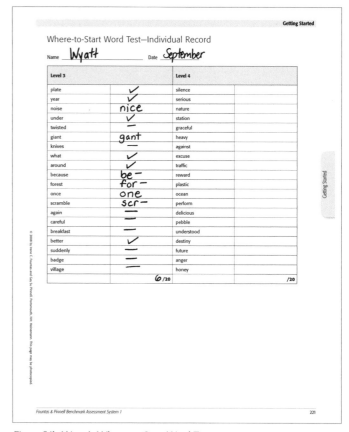

Figure 54a. Wyatt's Where-to-Start Word Test

Where-to-Start Word Test—Individual Record

Name Wyatt Date September

Level 3		Level 4	
plate	✓	silence	
year	✓	serious	
noise	nice	nature	
under	✓	station	
twisted	—	graceful	
giant	gant	heavy	
knives	—	against	
what	✓	excuse	
around	✓	traffic	
because	be–	reward	
forest	for–	plastic	
once	one	ocean	
scramble	scr–	perform	
again	—	delicious	
careful	—	pebble	
breakfast	—	understood	
better	✓	destiny	
suddenly	—	future	
badge	—	anger	
village	—	honey	
	6/20		/20

Figure 54b. Wyatt's Where-to-Start Word Test

Level H — Benchmark Independent

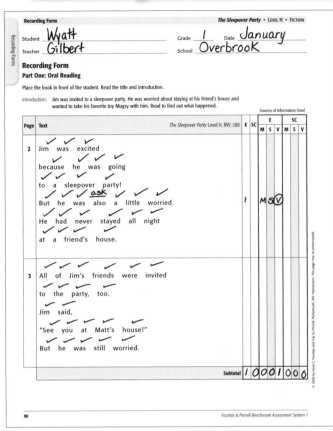

Figure 55a. Wyatt's Recording Form, level H

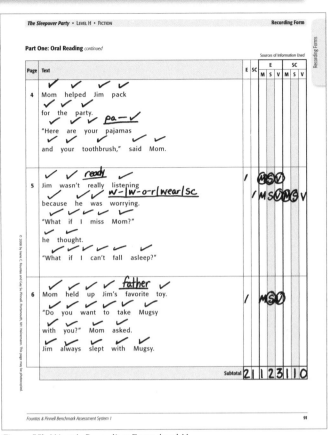

Figure 55b. Wyatt's Recording Form, level H

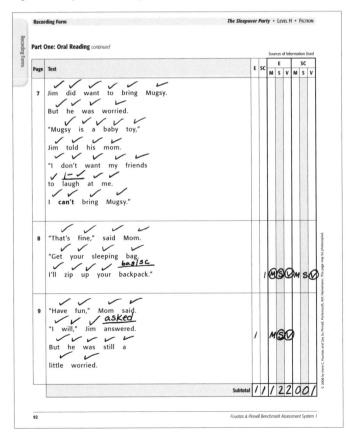

Figure 55c. Wyatt's Recording Form, level H

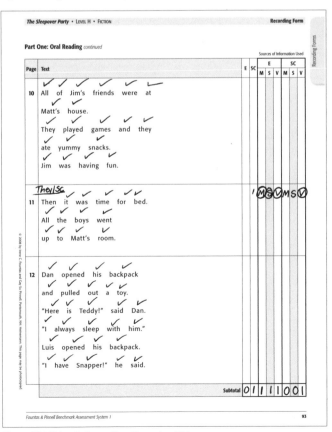

Figure 55d. Wyatt's Recording Form, level H

Level H — Benchmark Independent *(continued)*

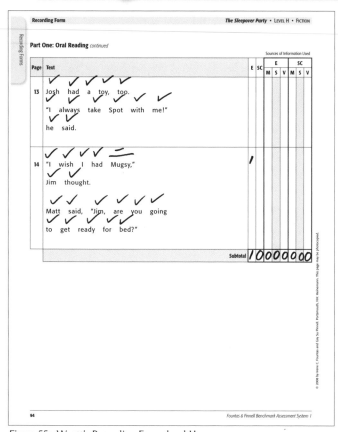

Figure 55e. Wyatt's Recording Form, level H

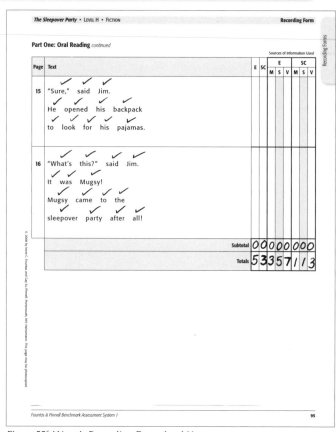

Figure 55f. Wyatt's Recording Form, level H

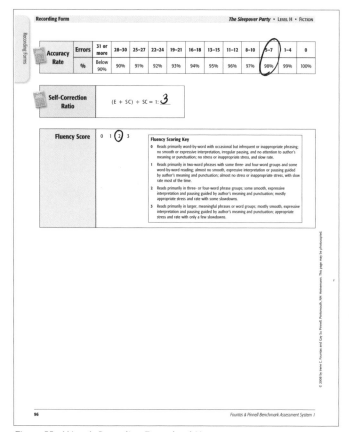

Figure 55g. Wyatt's Recording Form, level H

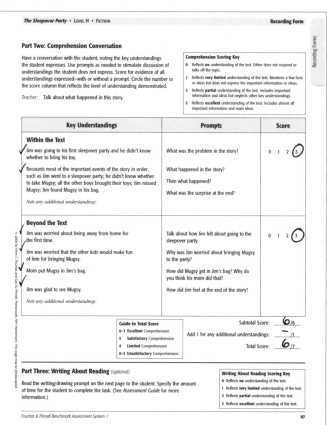

Figure 55h. Wyatt's Recording Form, level H

Level I — Benchmark Instructional

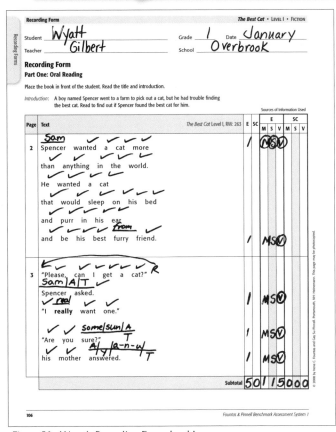

Figure 56a. Wyatt's Recording Form, level I

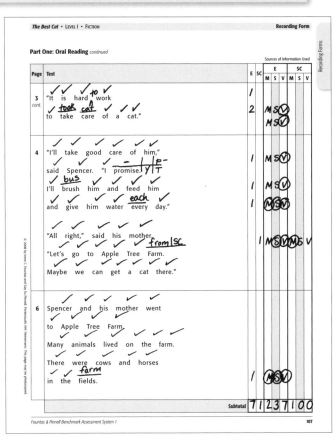

Figure 56b. Wyatt's Recording Form, level I

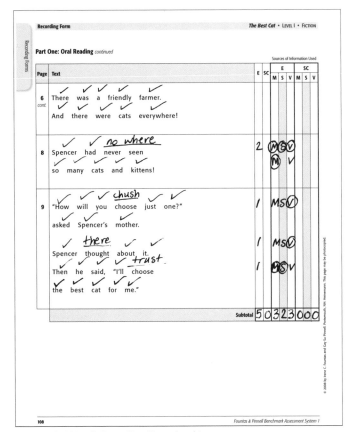

Figure 56c. Wyatt's Recording Form, level I

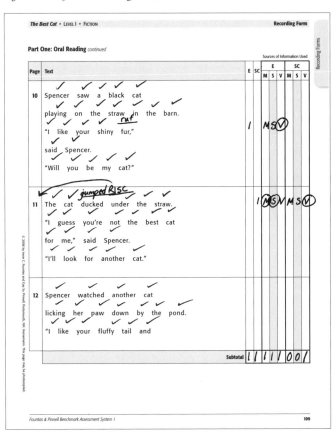

Figure 56d. Wyatt's Recording Form, level I

Level 1 — Benchmark Instructional (continued)

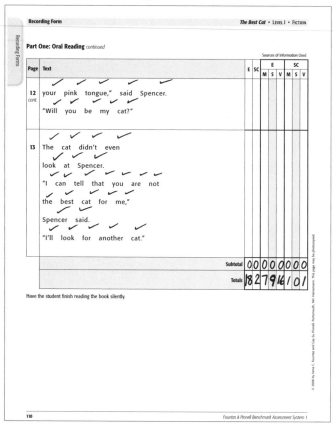

Figure 56e. Wyatt's Recording Form, level I

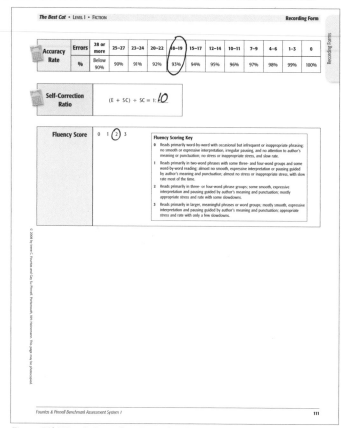

Figure 56f. Wyatt's Recording Form, level I

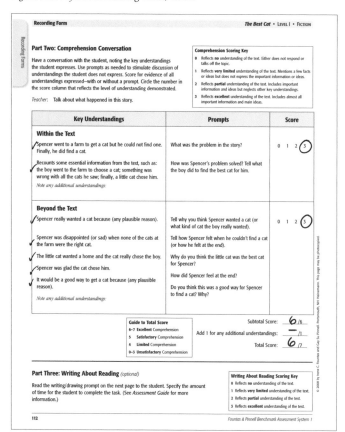

Figure 56g. Wyatt's Recording Form, level I

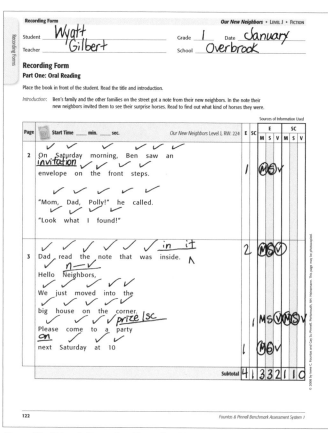

Figure 57a. Wyatt's Recording Form, level J

Level J — Hard Text

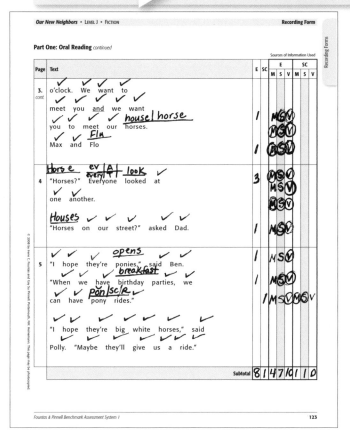

Figure 57b. Wyatt's Recording Form, level J

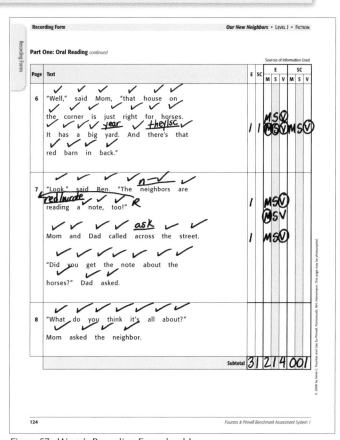

Figure 57c. Wyatt's Recording Form, level J

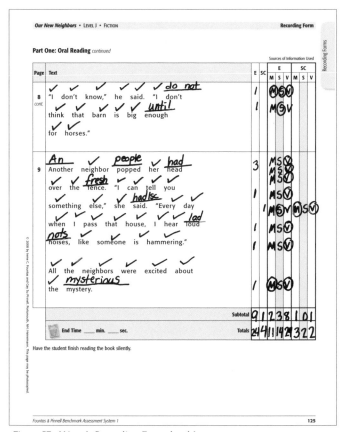

Figure 57e. Wyatt's Recording Form, level J

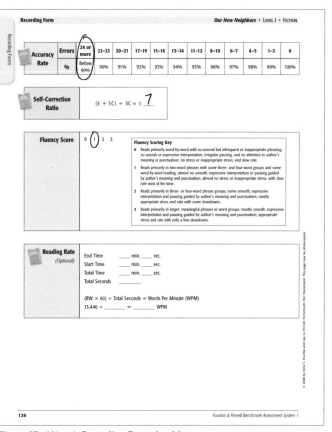

Figure 57g. Wyatt's Recording Form, level J

Level J — Hard Text (continued)

Our New Neighbors • LEVEL J • FICTION   Recording Form

Part Two: Comprehension Conversation

Have a conversation with the student, noting the key understandings the student expresses. Use prompts as needed to stimulate discussion of understandings the student does not express. Score for evidence of all understandings expressed—with or without a prompt. Circle the number in the score column that reflects the level of understanding demonstrated.

Teacher: Talk about what happened in this story.

Comprehension Scoring Key

0 Reflects **no** understanding of the text. Either does not respond or talks off the topic.

1 Reflects **very limited** understanding of the text. Mentions a few facts or ideas but does not express the important information or ideas.

2 Reflects **partial** understanding of the text. Includes important information and ideas but neglects other key understandings.

3 Reflects **excellent** understanding of the text. Includes almost all important information and main ideas.

Key Understandings	Prompts	Score
Within the Text Recounts most of the important events such as: the new neighbors invited everyone to see their horses; everyone was asking what kind of horses the neighbors had; the horses turned out to be a merry-go-round (or carousel). *Note any additional understandings:*	What was the mystery in the story? What did the new neighbors do to get everyone interested in their horses? What happened when people got the note? What happened at the end?	0 1 2 ③
Beyond the Text The new neighbors wanted to surprise everyone so they kept the horses a secret. Everyone was wondering about the horses and imagining the kinds of horses they were. Clues before the last page are: "loud hammering noises," "music playing," "two horses going up and two going down," "four horses going around and around". *Note any additional understandings:* *Remembered a carousel he rode on.*	Why did the new neighbors keep the horses a secret? What were the people in the neighborhood thinking about the horses? There were a few clues that might have helped you guess what kind of horses were in the barn. Can you think of any?	0 ① 2 3

Continued on next page.

Process broke down on hard text.

Fountas & Pinnell Benchmark Assessment System 1   127

Figure 57f. Wyatt's Recording Form, level J

Recording Form   **Our New Neighbors** • LEVEL J • FICTION

Part Two: Comprehension Conversation *continued*

Guide to Total Score	
6–7	**Excellent** Comprehension
5	**Satisfactory** Comprehension
4	**Limited** Comprehension
0–3	**Unsatisfactory** Comprehension

Subtotal Score: **3** /6

Add 1 for any additional understandings: **1** /1

Total Score: **4** /7

Part Three: Writing About Reading *(optional)*

Read the writing/drawing prompt on the next page to the student. Specify the amount of time for the student to complete the task. (See *Assessment Guide* for more information.)

Writing About Reading Scoring Key

0 Reflects **no** understanding of the text.

1 Reflects **very limited** understanding of the text.

2 Reflects **partial** understanding of the text.

3 Reflects **excellent** understanding of the text.

128   Fountas & Pinnell Benchmark Assessment System 1

Figure 57g. Wyatt's Recording Form, level J

Summary Forms

Benchmark Independent Level*	H
Benchmark Instructional Level**	I
Recommended Placement Level	J

Student: **Wyatt**   Grade: **1**   Date: **January**

Teacher: **Gilbert**   School: **Overbrook**

Assessment Summary Form

List the titles read by the student from lowest to highest level.

Title	System 1 or 2	Fiction/Nonfiction	Level	Accuracy	Comprehension	Independent* (check one)	Instructional** (check one)	Self-Correction	Fluency (levels C–Z)	Rate (levels J–Z) (optional)	Writing About Reading (optional)
The Sleepover Party	1	F	H	98	6	✓		1:3	2	—	
The Best Cat	1	F	I	94	6		✓	1:10	2		
Our New Neighbors	1	F	J	89	5			1:7	1	—	

*Independent Level:

Levels A–K: Highest level read with 95–100% accuracy and excellent or satisfactory comprehension.

Levels L–Z: Highest level read with 98–100% accuracy and excellent or satisfactory comprehension.

**Instructional Level

Levels A–K: Highest level read with 90–94% accuracy and excellent or satisfactory comprehension or 95–100% accuracy and limited comprehension.

Levels L–Z: Highest level read with 95–97% accuracy and excellent or satisfactory comprehension or 98–100% accuracy and limited comprehension.

Comprehension	
Levels A–K	Levels L–Z
6–7 Excellent	9–10 Excellent
5 Satisfactory	7–8 Satisfactory
4 Limited	5–6 Limited
0–3 Unsatisfactory	0–4 Unsatisfactory

Additional Comments:	Instructional Implications:

Fountas & Pinnell Benchmark Assessment System 1   203

Figure 58. Wyatt's Assessment Summary

The Best Cat • LEVEL I • FICTION   Recording Form

Student: **Wyatt**   Grade: **1**   Date: _____

Write about Spencer and how he found the best cat. You can draw a picture to go with your writing.

Fountas & Pinnell Benchmark Assessment System 1   113

Figure 59. Wyatt's writing

Mr. Gilbert Talks About Wyatt

I was impressed with Wyatt's ability to read words in isolation on the Where-to-Start Word Test. Since he is reading only at level G in the classroom, I started him at that point in the benchmark testing. He read *Bubbles* very easily with 100% accuracy. I was also surprised that *The Sleepover Party* was easy for him. His reading was not completely fluent, but he did have some phrases and many stretches of fluent reading.

When we went on to *The Best Cat*, I was again surprised. He could read this text at an instructional level, and I noticed that he knows many high-frequency words. He can also use visual features of words to solve them. I was concerned, though, that he seemed to go right on when his errors didn't make sense. I did notice that he can self-correct; for example, when he read *jumped* for *ducked*, he self-corrected immediately, right at the point of error; but other errors were just left. For example, he read "Spencer there about it" instead of "Spencer thought about it." I would have liked for him to notice this mismatch, because it didn't make sense.

His reading of *Our New Neighbors* was not accurate enough, but he did get the gist of the story. Here, again, he seems to make errors without noticing when he is losing meaning. I am wondering if he thinks he should just "know" every word and when he encounters a new one, he just takes a guess at it without searching for different sources of information. For example, saying *house* for *horse* does not make sense with the entire story, but Wyatt did not stop to distinguish between the two easy words.

An interesting error was *opens* for *ponies*. This error did not make sense and did not fit with language structure in the sentence: "'I hope they're ponies,' said Ben." At first I thought this error did not fit visually, but then I noticed that *opens* has five of the same letters that are in *ponies*—just turned around a bit. This makes me wonder if Wyatt is consistently looking at words left to right or if he is simply looking at the word as a whole. I will need to watch closely for this.

I am going to place Wyatt instructionally at a level J. Given his performance on level I and the way he was processing the text at level J, I think instruction will provide the necessary support for him to demonstrate more effective reading behaviors. Wyatt needs a good introduction to the text and to be prompted to monitor his reading as to whether it "makes sense" and "sounds right." He also needs discussion of the story afterward and many opportunities to write about reading. I would particularly like to see him reach for some of the underlying ideas and reflect them in writing.

Figure 60. Mr. Gilbert's comments about Wyatt's reading

Continued on next page

Looking at the continuum for level J, I have selected these goals as being important for Wyatt:

▸ demonstrate knowledge of flexible ways to solve words (other than first letter)

▸ self-correct at point of error

▸ reread to confirm word solving by checking other sources of information

▸ use multiple sources of information to monitor and self-correct

▸ break down a longer word into syllables in order to decode manageable units

▸ identify important ideas in a text and report them in an organized way

▸ make predictions based on personal experiences, content knowledge, and knowledge of similar texts

▸ summarize a longer narrative text with multiple episodes

▸ through talk or writing, demonstrate learning new content from reading

▸ understand the problem of a story and its solution

▸ notice and discuss aspects of genres—fiction and nonfiction and realistic stories and fantasy

As mentioned above, I am concerned that Wyatt may be using a narrow range of word-solving strategies. He has knowledge of many high-frequency words, but when he approaches unfamiliar words, I would like for him to become more flexible—using word parts and connecting words that are similar as well as using letter-sound relationships. I also want to be sure that he is attending to words from left to right. During individual conferences and in the word work that follows guided reading, I plan to engage Wyatt in these areas:

▸ solve words using letter-sound analysis from left to right (white board demonstration; magnet letters; student white boards)

▸ take apart more complex compound words (white board demonstration)

▸ change words to make more complex plurals (add *es*; white board demonstrations; student white boards)

▸ change words to add inflectional endings (endings, prefixes)

Figure 60. Mr. Gilbert's comments about Wyatt's reading (*continued*)

Sharla, Grade 2 Student

In the figures on the following pages, you see Sharla's Where-to-Start Word Test (Figure 61), Recording Forms for levels L, M, and N (Figures 62, 63, 64), and her Assessment Summary (Figure 65).

Sharla scored 20 on level 1, 19 on level 2, and 15 on level 3 of the Where-to-Start Word Test. The screening revealed that she knew many high-frequency words as well as many two-syllable words. Her substitutions (*tore/twisted*, and *fork/forest*, for example) revealed her ability to use letter-sound relationships. In cases where the word was probably unknown, she was able to produce a facsimile—for example, pronouncing *badge* with a long *a* sound.

Oral Reading. Sharla read *Dog Stories*, level L fiction, at 98% accuracy and her fluency rating was 1. She then read *The Thing About Nathan* at 95% accuracy, with a fluency rating of 2. She read *The Big Snow* at 91% accuracy, with a fluency rating of 1. Since this was the ending text in the Benchmark 1 series, no further testing was done, but considering Sharla's performance on *The Big Snow*, this level could be considered "hard" because she read with low fluency and had difficulty demonstrating comprehension.

When Sharla read *Dog Stories*, she demonstrated that she could take words apart to solve them (*ex-it-ed*, self-corrected on page 2 and *fav-favorite* on page 5). She self-corrected after substituting *fan* for *favorite*, indicating that she can use several sources of information—the spelling and length of the word as well as meaning—in order to correct. As easy as this text was for Sharla, we would have liked to see a higher rating on fluency. Additionally, her responses during the comprehension conversation indicated only vague understandings about the plot. It may be that the story did not engage the reader, since the most important comment was, "It could really happen." Her comprehension score was 5 of the 10 possible points, indicating limited comprehension.

Sharla read *The Thing About Nathan* at 95% accuracy, and this time scored 9 out of 10 points on comprehension. She stated that "Nathan and William are opposites" and hypothesized that "Maybe Hanna and Jerry are opposites too." This text appeared to engage the reader. She read with high accuracy, using all sources of information most of the time. For example, she demonstrated the use of multiple cues. She said *cleaning* for *clean* and then self-corrected to accurately read the word. She self-corrected her substitution of *dream* for *drives* and *tried* for *trade*. Sharla's self-corrections were close to the point of error, indicating quick processing.

On unfamiliar words, Sharla demonstrated her ability to make attempts at words based on her knowledge of letter-sound relationships (for example, *dream* for *drives* and *middle* for *model*). In these cases, it is not clear whether the word was in Sharla's oral vocabulary. There was little evidence that she was searching for what would make sense or sound right in the sentence. Occasionally, she made a substitution (for example, *kittens* for *kits*) that did not make sense and was left uncorrected.

Sharla read *The Big Snow* at 91% accuracy with a score of 1 on fluency. On this text, her comprehension score was 5 of 10, indicating limited comprehension. She was able to relate details from the text and to infer Patrick's feelings at the beginning and ending of the story. Her error and self-correction pattern indicates a flexible use of many sources of information. She demonstrated that she could take apart multisyllable words like *elevator* (*el-va-elevator*) on the run while reading continuous text. On the other hand, when Sharla had too much problem solving to do, she relied on letter-sound information only. For example, she read "Patrick took off his soggy coat" as "Patrick took off his sag coat." The fact that the process broke down occasionally during her reading of the text was probably related to the fluency score of only 1. She exhibited a self-correction ratio of 1:0.

Comprehension Conversation. During the comprehension conversation, Sharla demonstrated the ability to remember details from the story but showed only a superficial ability to infer the feelings of the characters and talk about the structure of the text. However, Sharla's responses were good enough to show that she was able to process this text with understanding. In Figure 66, Sharla's teacher, Mrs. Ford, talks about Sharla's reading.

Getting Started

Where-to-Start Word Test—Individual Record

Name Sharla Date September

Beginning		Level 1		Level 2	
me		jump	✓	want	✓
I		here	✓	friend	✓
can		little	✓	puppy	✓
to		went	✓	basket	—
my		has	✓	could	✓
we		girl	✓	dark	✓
in		will	✓	down	✓
like		have	✓	road	✓
it		ball	✓	plant	✓
up		make	✓	away	✓
mom		play	✓	morning	✓
the		was	✓	three	✓
and		bike	✓	cool	✓
he		with	✓	drop	✓
look		they	✓	grass	✓
is		this	✓	when	✓
see		bed	✓	first	✓
come		feet	✓	train	✓
get		one	✓	queen	✓
at		said	✓	scream	✓
	/20		20/20		19/20

Getting Started

220 *Fountas & Pinnell Benchmark Assessment System 1*

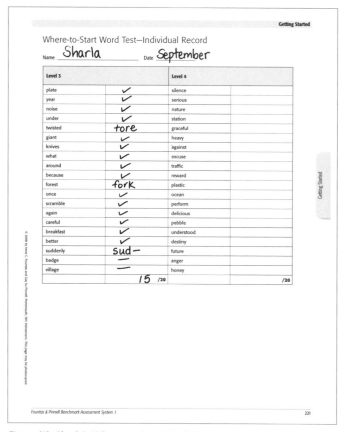

Figure 61a. Sharla's Where-to-Start Word Test

Getting Started

Where-to-Start Word Test—Individual Record

Name Sharla Date September

Level 3		Level 4	
plate	✓	silence	
year	✓	serious	
noise	✓	nature	
under	✓	station	
twisted	tore	graceful	
giant	✓	heavy	
knives	✓	against	
what	✓	excuse	
around	✓	traffic	
because	✓	reward	
forest	fork	plastic	
once	✓	ocean	
scramble	✓	perform	
again	✓	delicious	
careful	✓	pebble	
breakfast	✓	understood	
better	✓	destiny	
suddenly	sud–	future	
badge	—	anger	
village	—	honey	
	15 /20		/20

Getting Started

Fountas & Pinnell Benchmark Assessment System 1 221

Figure 61b. Sharla's Where-to-Start Word Test

Level L — Benchmark Independent

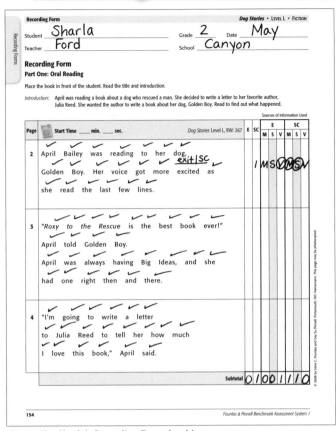

Figure 62a. Sharla's Recording Form, level L

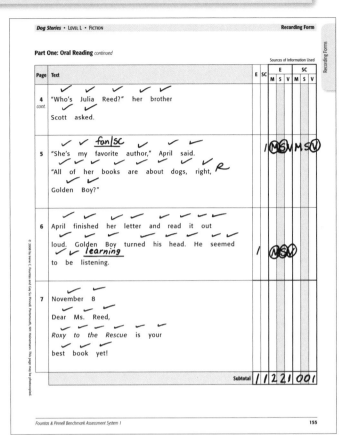

Figure 62b. Sharla's Recording Form, level L

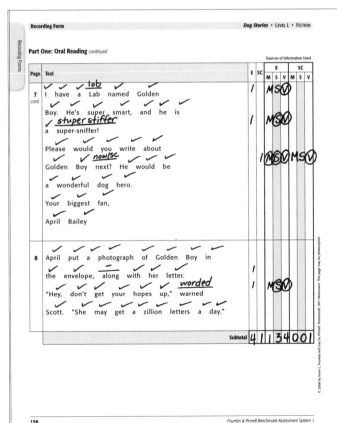

Figure 62c. Sharla's Recording Form, level L

Figure 62d. Sharla's Recording Form, level L

Level L — Benchmark Independent *(continued)*

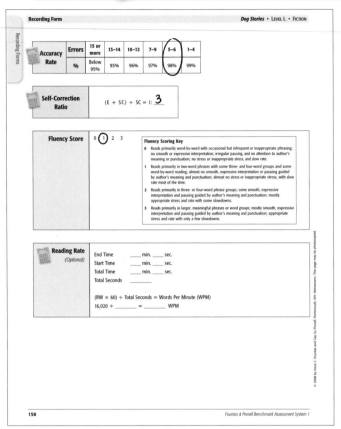

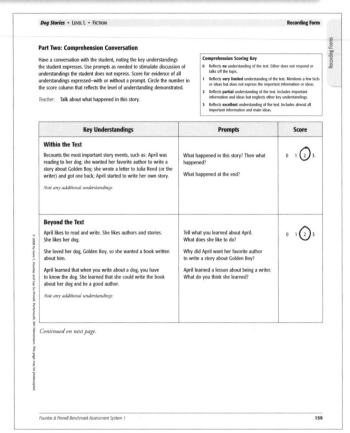

Figure 62e. Sharla's Recording Form, level L

Figure 62f. Sharla's Recording Form, level L

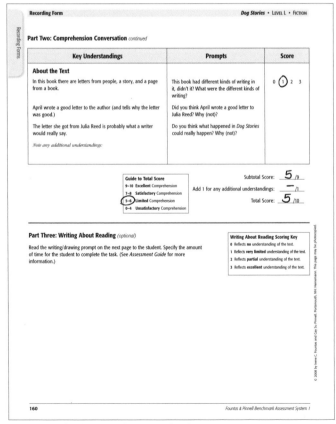

Figure 62g. Sharla's Recording Form, level L

Level M — Benchmark Instructional

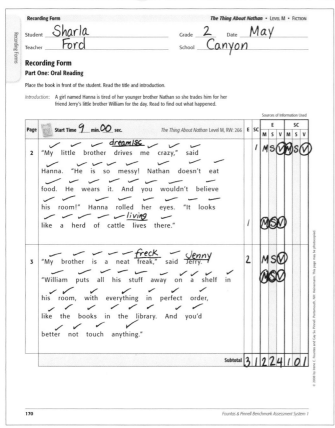

Figure 63a. Sharla's Recording Form, level M

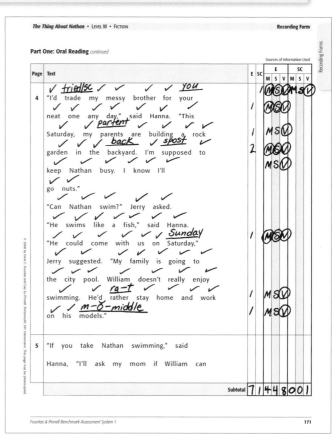

Figure 63b. Sharla's Recording Form, level M

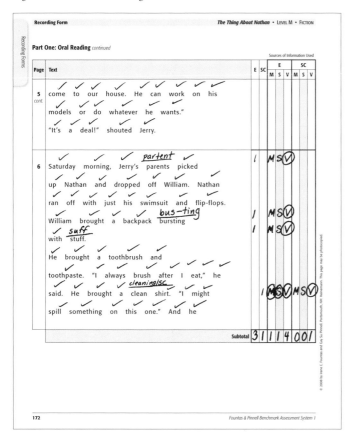

Figure 63c. Sharla's Recording Form, level M

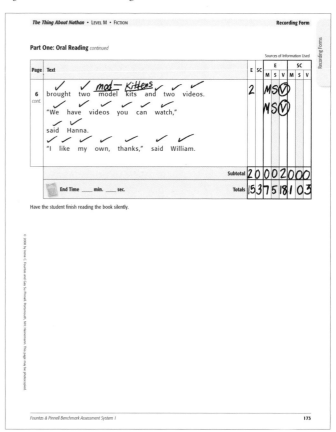

Figure 63d. Sharla's Recording Form, level M

Level M — Benchmark Instructional (*continued*)

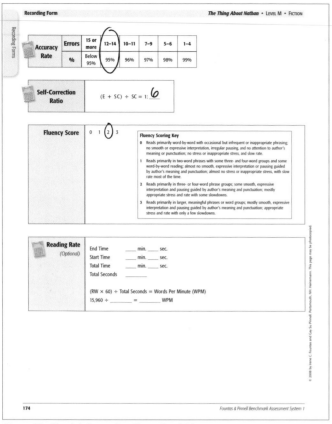

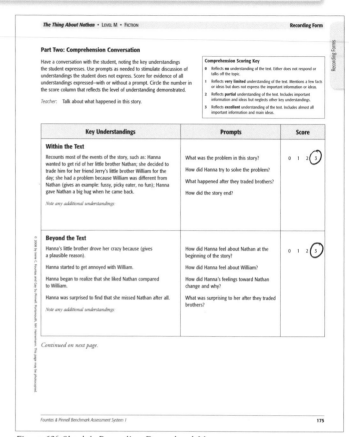

Figure 63e. Sharla's Recording Form, level M

Figure 63f. Sharla's Recording Form, level M

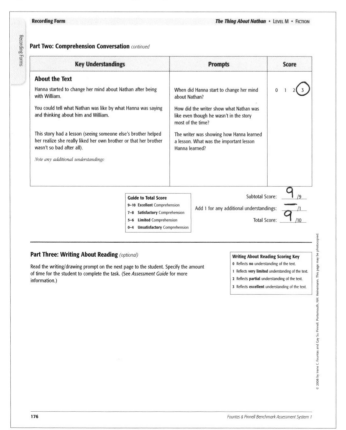

Figure 63g. Sharla's Recording Form, level M

Level N — Hard Text

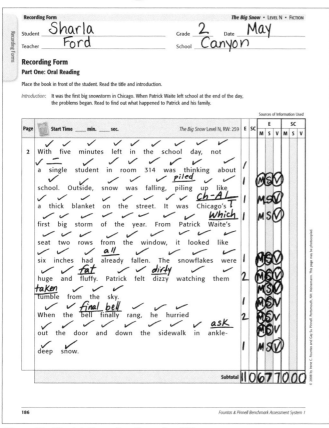

Figure 64a. Sharla's Recording Form, level N

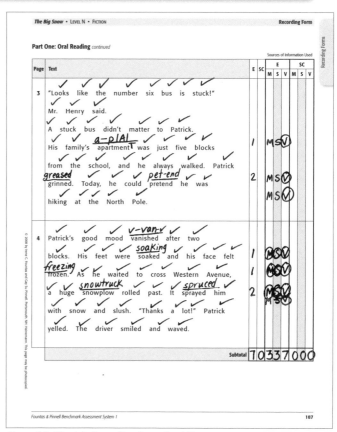

Figure 64b. Sharla's Recording Form, level N

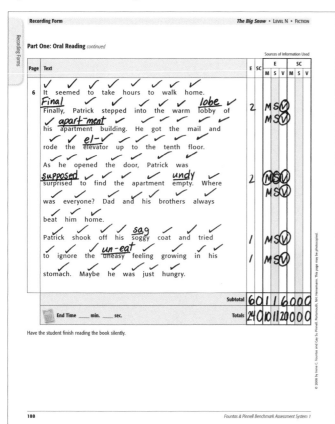

Figure 64c. Sharla's Recording Form, level N

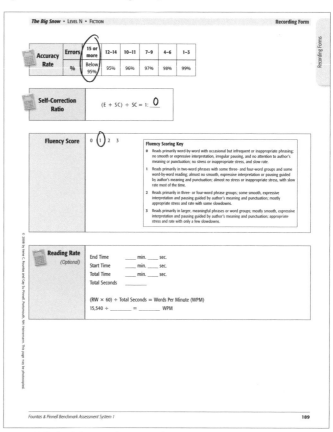

Figure 64d. Sharla's Recording Form, level N

Level N — Hard Text (*continued*)

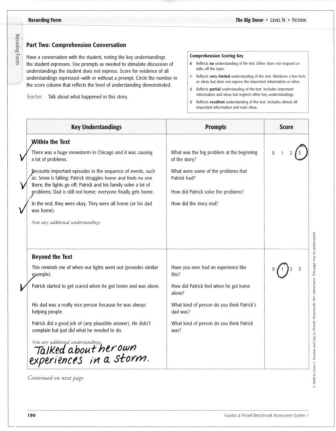

Figure 64e. Sharla's Recording Form, level N

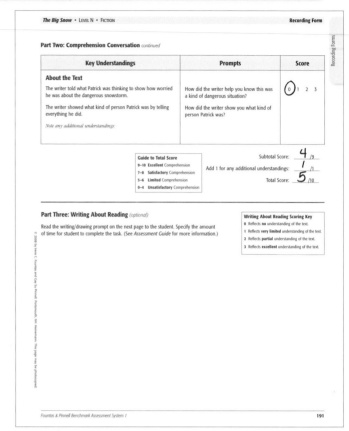

Figure 64f. Sharla's Recording Form, level N

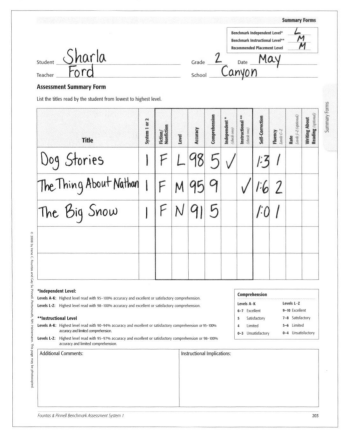

Figure 65. Sharla's Assessment Summary

Mrs. Ford Talks About Sharla

Sharla is doing well as a second-grade reader. She read *Dog Stories* at an independent reading level and *The Thing About Nathan* at an instructional level. On all of these texts, Sharla showed that she knows and recognizes a great many words automatically. Also, she can definitely decode words on the run while reading continuous text. I noticed that she had difficulty with the word *excited* in *Dog Stories*. She made a good attempt, but I would have liked to see her work at it a little more. She read the word *worded* for *warned*, which actually matches the language structure, although not the meaning. I was most concerned that she had a fluency rating of 1. This text was not hard for her, so I would have expected more fluency. On the other hand, this was a reading of an unseen text, so she might do much better on the second reading or with a good introduction to the text. *Dog Stories* is definitely an independent reading level for her.

She read *The Thing About Nathan* at 95% accuracy, indicating that this text was at an instructional level for her. Her fluency rate was 2. I was impressed that her comprehension level was 9 out of 10, indicating that she had very good understanding (thinking within, beyond, and about the text). Her reading behavior indicates a general pattern to using all information sources in an orchestrated way. For example, she read "I'd tried my messy brother" for "I'd trade my messy brother" on page 4, but then self-corrected. This error and self-correction behavior indicates that she was processing the text as language, using the meaning and language structure as well as visual information. On this text, Sharla consistently monitored her own reading and made self-corrections as appropriate.

The comprehension conversation indicated that Sharla was able to recall important details from the text and to say that the two boys, William and Nathan, were opposites. She also speculated that Jerry and Hanna might be opposites. Her score on comprehension was 9 of 10.

Sharla read *The Big Snow* at below 95% accuracy. She was able to recount some details from the text but was not able to infer the characters' feelings and causes. Her comprehension score was 5 of 10. Her reading indicated the knowledge of a great many high-frequency words. Also, error behavior indicated the search for and use of many different sources of information.

I think that level M is the placement level for Sharla. She needs more opportunities to discuss texts and self-monitor her reading to be sure it makes sense. It may be that she is more focused on solving words and accuracy than on actively thinking about the text, and her comprehension suffered. I would like her to be more thoughtful about the texts that she reads.

Figure 66. Mrs. Ford's comments about Sharla's reading

Continued on next page

Looking at the A–N literacy learning continuum, I have selected the following goals for Sharla:

- when reading aloud, self-correct intonation when it does not reflect the meaning

- consistently check on understanding and search for information when meaning breaks down

- search for information in graphics (simple diagrams, illustrations with labels, maps, charts)

- make a wide range of predictions based on personal experiences, content knowledge, and knowledge of similar texts

- make predictions as to the solution of the problem in the story and support them with evidence from the text

- make connections between the text and other texts that have been read or heard

- differentiate between what is already known and new information

- infer the big ideas or theses of a text

- demonstrate, through talk or writing, understanding of characters (using evidence from the text)

- demonstrate how a text is organized using a diagram

- notice and interpret figurative language and discuss how it adds to the meaning or enjoyment of a text

- understand the relationships between the setting and the plot of a story

- infer causes of problems or of outcomes in fiction and nonfiction texts

Figure 66. Mrs. Ford's comments about Sharla's reading (*continued*)

Selena, Grade 1 English Language Learner

In Figures 67 and 68, starting on page 100, you see two Recording Forms for Selena. She is an English language learner who is new to the school, about the middle of grade 1.

Selena was a new English speaker when she moved to the school in October. Since then, she has been making progress in oral control of English and also in reading and writing. Her school does not provide bilingual education, but her teacher, Mr. Foster, has given her both small-group instruction and some individual help.

Oral Reading. Selena read four texts, *Socks* (level C), *The Nice Little House* (level D), *The Zoo* (level E), and *The Loose Tooth* (level E). At levels C and D, Selena read with relatively high accuracy. When reading *Socks* (Figure 67), Selena substituted *sleep* for *sleeping* and *say* for *said* several times without stopping or appealing. These repeated errors led her teacher to hypothesize that they might be related to language proficiency. Selena spontaneously self-corrected *sleeping* on page 8, competently taking it apart and appearing to notice the ending, and she read the word accurately after that. When she noticed the mismatch on *said* on page 8, she appealed and was told the word. After that she read it accurately. She also had trouble with the word *window*, which Mr. Foster thought might also be related to language. Her reading of *Socks* was in the instructional range for accuracy, although on the low side. The teacher engaged her in the comprehension conversation.

In discussing *Socks*, Selena was able to report the general theme of the story (that Socks was a very sleepy cat and the girl was trying to get her to wake up) and tell that the girl finally made the cat wake up by getting some food. The teacher decided that her comprehension was satisfactory.

Moving on to the next level, Selena read *The Nice Little House* (Figure 68) with an accu-racy rate of 92%. With this accuracy rating, the teacher wondered if the level would be easy for her. He also noticed that she read *say* for *said* again and then self-corrected. Maybe the word was familiar from her reading of *Socks*. On page 2, she seemed simply to "sound out" *nice*, pronouncing it in the way she might in her native language; on page 4, she began the word but then appealed, indicating she was aware of the error and probably that the text was not making sense to her. Mr. Foster also noticed that she read *little* for *big* at the end of the story, possibly just following the pattern without notic-ing a word that she actually knew how to read. Finally, he thought that the language structure ("What a nice little house") might be difficult for Selena beyond the individual words. This expression is not one she would have used in her current command of oral English. When the structure is particularly difficult for a reader, it is hard to process the text as language, and it may not make sense. The reader is reduced to word calling. This can happen to any reader, even those with English as a first language.

When Mr. Foster engaged Selena in the comprehension conversation, he was con-cerned. Even though her accuracy was high, she could say only that animals had gone into a house. She was not sure why they left and said that the skunk was "sad" at the end because the others were gone. These misun-derstandings, again, might be related to lan-guage. But the teacher determined that her comprehension was barely satisfactory. This reading indicated that the text was too hard. Realizing that decision making is tricky when you are considering language proficiency, the teacher decided to go on to the next level.

Selena's accuracy rate on *The Zoo* was low, but Mr. Foster went on to have her read the fic-tion text, *The Loose Tooth*, at that level because he thought Selena might not have known the names of animals. Since she missed almost all of them, Mr. Foster thought her problem was related to English labels. But it was clear that *The Loose Tooth* was also too difficult, so they finished that text together.

After looking across the readings of *Socks* and *The Little House*, Mr. Foster reflected on Selena's progress. He decided that the appropriate Benchmark Instructional level for Selena was C and her Benchmark Independent level was B. However, she was making very good progress, and he planned to move her quickly to level D. The teacher decided that within the next month, Selena would need:

▶ a great deal of independent reading at levels A, B, and within a short time C in order to build her reading vocabulary

▶ many opportunities to talk about texts that are within her range for accuracy and understanding

▶ small-group instruction at level C, moving to D within a short period of time, with specific support in vocabulary and language structure

▶ many opportunities to hear written language read aloud in order to become more familiar with the structure of sentences as well as the structure of stories

▶ many opportunities to discuss stories that she has heard read aloud

Some considerations for assessing English language learners' reading are summarized in Figure 69.

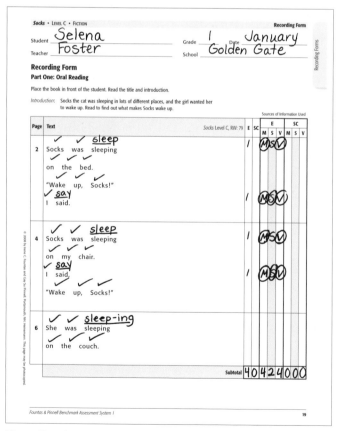

Figure 67a. Selena's Recording Form, level C

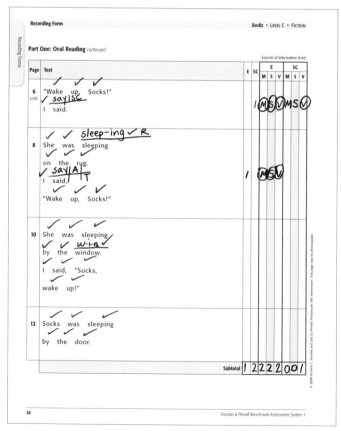

Figure 67b. Selena's Recording Form, level C

Level C *(continued)* and Level D

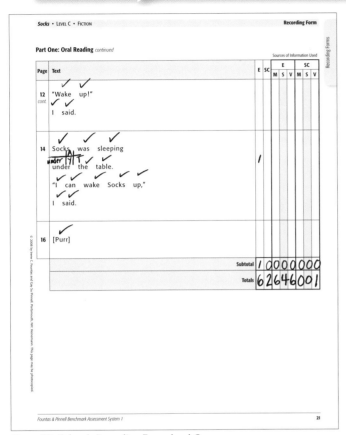

Figure 67c. Selena's Recording Form, level C

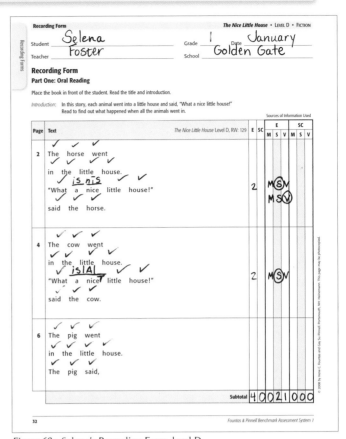

Figure 68a. Selena's Recording Form, level D

Figure 68b. Selena's Recording Form, level D

Figure 68c. Selena's Recording Form, level D

Level D (continued)

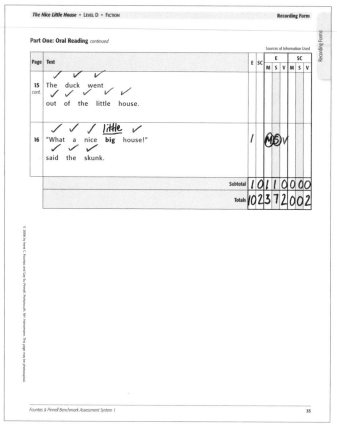

Figure 68d. Selena's Recording Form, level D

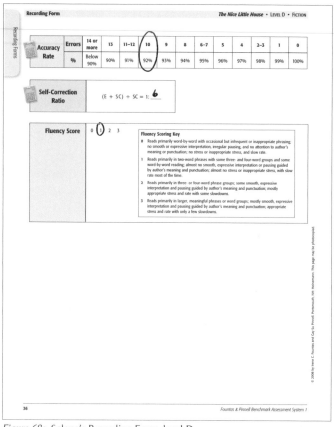

Figure 68e. Selena's Recording Form, level D

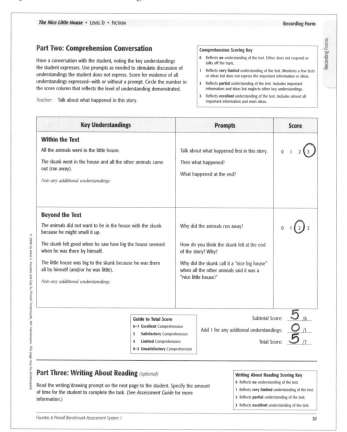

Figure 68f. Selena's Recording Form, level D

Figure 68g. Selena's Recording Form, level D

English Language Learners: Considerations for Assessment of Reading	
Administration	▷ Follow your district policy regarding the level of English proficiency required for standardized assessment.
	▷ Administer the assessment with the standardized procedures. If a student does not understand directions or a question, paraphrase so the student will know what is required.
	▷ Discontinue the student's reading of a benchmark book when it is clearly too difficult.
Coding and scoring	▷ Code the reading using the standard conventions.
	▷ If the errors that a student makes appear to be related to the influence of the student's first language, make a quick note on the Recording Form. For example, the student might apply the rules of syntax from the first language or have a particular way of enunciating the sounds in a word.
	▷ In general, errors related to syntax are counted as errors. Use judgment in counting slight variations in pronunciation as errors; they might be dialect differences.
	▷ In addition to coding behaviors, you can make some quick notes on the form to help you remember any difficulties you think are due to the student's first language. Also, make some notes on phrasing and fluency.
Analysis	▷ Analyze the student's use of sources of information using the standardized procedures.
	▷ Make notes on your record when you think an error is related to a difference in the student's background knowledge, cultural knowledge, control of language structure, or dialect.
Fluency	▷ Take into account the fact that there may be some variation in stress and intonation based on the way a student speaks English orally.
	▷ Take into account that some pauses may be related not only to solving the word but also to recalling what the English word means.
Comprehension	▷ Consider the content of a particular text in your interpretation.
	▷ Realize that a student may lack the background knowledge or evidence a difference in cultural knowledge.
	▷ Realize that some discrepancy may not be reading comprehension as much as it is language proficiency.

Figure 69. Considerations for reading assessment with English language learners

Continued on next page

	English Language Learners: Considerations for Assessment of Reading *continued*
Interpretation of the assessment	▶ Oral language is an important factor in the reading process. If a student has never heard a word, it will be more difficult for her to read it. She will likely rely more on using the visual information only.
	▶ If a student does not use a particular language structure, it will be difficult for her to use the structure of the language to anticipate new words.
	▶ If the context of the text is not meaningful to the student, it will be more difficult for him to use meaning as a guide to problem solve the words in the text.
	▶ Avoid placing the student in texts that are too difficult. You do not want the English language learner to rely only on calling words with little attention to meaning.

Figure 69. Considerations for reading assessment with English language learners

Documenting Student Growth in Reading Over Time

One assessment conference with the Fountas & Pinnell Benchmark Assessment System represents a student's reading at one point in time. Using standardized procedures and multiple leveled texts, the conference provides a reliable picture of the student's reading strengths and weaknesses at that time. Benchmark assessments that are taken two or three times during a year provide a good picture of a student's progress in the instructional program. Nevertheless, benchmark assessment results must always be understood within the perspective of the ongoing observation you do every day during reading instruction, especially at early levels.

Young children change very rapidly during the early years of schooling. By using the benchmark assessment as a baseline, conducting informal observations, and coding oral reading on running records or reading records at specific intervals, you can track the growth of individuals over time and gain valuable instructional information. You can also identify students who are going off track and provide planned intervention.

In this section, we examine ways of looking at individual progress over time and monitoring adequate progress.

Looking at Individual Progress

The Assessment Summary forms in the *Assessment Forms* book and CD-ROM provide a place to record a student's Benchmark Independent and Benchmark Instructional levels. There are versions for recording scores two (Bi-annual Assessment Summary), three (Tri-annual Assessment Summary), or four (Quarterly Assessment Summary) times a year. (The *Data Management* CD-ROM will update this report from the data entered at individual conferences.) These scores plot a child's progress over time and provide a clear picture of how the educational system is bringing the student forward as a reader.

In addition, two reading graphs can chart an individual's reading progress. The Annual Record of Reading Progress provides opportunities for noting the levels from Benchmark Assessment conferences and interim running records. The date and title of the book with the accuracy rate of the reading are entered onto the form and a symbol is placed on a grid so that a line connecting the symbols provides a graph of progress. The Longitudinal Record of Reading Progress—found in the *Assessment Forms* book and CD-ROM as well as printed on the Student Folder—plots a student's Benchmark level (either Independent or Instructional) four times a year across all eight grades. The *Data Management* CD-ROM creates similar graphs once you've entered the data.

Monitoring Adequate Progress

With typical progress, we would expect kindergarten children to take on the very easy levels of text successfully; that is, by the end of the year they would be reading level B or C. And they would be independently reading these easy texts after an introduction, rather than experiencing them in shared reading four or five times. Even though these levels are easy, becoming able to process them effectively represents a large amount of learning. These young readers have figured out how print "works," learned some high-frequency words, and are processing texts as language.

Typically, first graders will move from level B or C to about level I or J within the school year. These levels are narrow and carefully defined to provide small steps. Across second grade, children usually read from about level H or I to level M or N. Of course, no child is "typical." One might be slow to take on reading but once she attends to it moves rapidly. Another may use language skillfully but need more time and teaching in order to effectively process visual information.

Your daily observations of reading behavior and systematic administration of the Benchmark Assessment System will help you to notice and document progress so that you can determine when children need intervention. For example, entering first graders who have participated in kindergarten and still know very little about print may need an extra "boost" in the form of one-to-one tutoring. Reading Recovery has an excellent record of research in helping first graders get back on track quickly. (See the What Works Clearinghouse, www.whatworks.ed.gov.) A first grader who is still reading around level D or E by March may need extra help in the form of tutoring or well-designed small-group intervention such as Leveled Literacy Intervention (Fountas and Pinnell, Heinemann, in press), a small-group supplementary intervention for children in kindergarten, grade 1, grade 2, or even higher, who are reading below grade level. A second grader who is reading on levels G or H will also need extra help to catch up with grade-level expectations. Systematic assessment at the beginning, middle, and end of the year will reveal students who are not making adequate progress and require intervention.

Some characteristics of effective interventions are:

▶ daily reading of continuous text at instructional level

▶ reading and rereading easier texts at independent level

▶ phonics and word work appropriate to the level

▶ writing in connection with reading

▶ intensive teaching by an individual with specialized skills

We do not recommend that students who are having difficulty be turned over to paraprofessionals or volunteers. These children need the most skilled teaching of all.

Case Study: Looking at One Reader at Three Points in Time

One advantage of using a benchmark system is that it allows you to document and analyze each child's progress over time. We want every student to develop a highly efficient, smoothly orchestrated reading process. Some do so rapidly, with little instruction; but most need the careful monitoring that will inform instruction.

Figures 70–77 on pages 110–115 show selected results from Kendra's assessment conferences in September, January, and June of first grade. Kendra showed many strengths on her literacy assessment as she entered first grade. As indicated by her Assessment Summary, she could read Level C at 97% accuracy with satisfactory comprehension (see Figure 70).

Kendra was not reading fluently at this level because she had just begun to track print with her eyes and was still occasionally using her finger to point at words. She monitored her reading closely, self-correcting one out of every two errors. Level C was a good independent reading level for her, meaning that she would be able to continue to expand her systems of strategic actions by reading many books at this level. Her instructional level was D (see Figure 71). She read *Our Teacher Mr. Brown* at 92% accuracy, although she was even less fluent than on level C.

We can see from her error behavior that Kendra was, again, closely monitoring her reading. She reread to solve words, searching to make all information sources fit. For example, on page 2, line 2, she made the first sound of *school* and then went back to the beginning of the line to reread, this time solving the word. On page 4, she made two errors (*is reading* for *reads*). Her reading made sense and sounded right, but when she saw the word *books,* she was cued by visual information to notice the error. She went back to the beginning of the line and reread to self-correct the two errors.

Several errors went unnoticed, but these, too, indicated that she was using meaning, language structure, and visual information. As she talked about the text, Kendra demonstrated that she had satisfactory comprehension, and she even mentioned a few other things that the children probably did at school (other than those in the book), giving her an extra point for additional understandings. Her score was 7.

When she attempted the level E text, *The Loose Tooth,* Kendra demonstrated good problem solving and knowledge of high-frequency words; however, this text was too difficult. She read it at 88% accuracy with unsatisfactory comprehension; the process had broken down. Kendra began to participate in small-group instruction at a placement level of D.

In Figure 72, you see Kendra's mid-year assessment summary. We can see progress.

She read *From Nest to Bird,* level F, at 97% accuracy with satisfactory comprehension; however, the teacher noted that her comments did not indicate that she was actively thinking beyond the text. Her score was 5, just at "satisfactory level." Also, her fluency was still low. At this level and with such high accuracy, we would expect Kendra to demonstrate better phrasing, intonation, and stress on words.

On *Bedtime for Nick,* level G (see Figure 73), Kendra read with 94% accuracy.

She knew many high-frequency words; her errors indicated that she was using meaning, language structure, and visual information. She was doing a great deal of rereading and careful self-monitoring; she seemed to concentrate on getting every word right, and her fluency was low. Sometimes she made errors that indicated she was not using multiple sources of information, and she appealed several times.

Kendra's comprehension on this level G text was satisfactory, which puzzled the teacher. The teacher's hypothesis was that Kendra was working so carefully to solve words that she was not attending enough to meaning and not processing fluently. When Kendra moved to the next level, H, the process fell apart. Her self-correction rate was only 1:11; her comprehension was limited, and her fluency was scored as 0.

This assessment indicated a placement level of F (her independent level) for a week or two to allow Kendra and some of her other classmates to experience strong instruction in fluency and phrasing, as well as opportunities to enter into conversation and write or draw about their reading. They moved quickly to level G, but the key was to have these students process texts that were easy enough to free them to give attention to meaning and to the processing of language. Meanwhile, this small group continued to work with letters, sounds, and words to make their word solving quick and automatic.

At the end of the year, Kendra read level I, *The Best Cat,* at 98% accuracy (see Figure 74).

Her fluency had dramatically improved, with a score of 3 on her reading of this level I text; and even more important, her comprehension was excellent. She read *More Than a Pet,* level J, with accuracy of 95%, excellent comprehension, and a fluency rating of 2. She read level K, *Edwin's Haircut,* at 94% accuracy with satisfactory comprehension, and a fluency rating of 2 (Figure 75). These assessments indicated that Kendra was reading words in phrases most of the time, even on texts that were more difficult.

She read *Dog Stories,* level L, at 91% accuracy. Remember that a higher criterion is employed at level L, so this reading indicated that the text was too hard for her. Also, her comprehension was unsatisfactory.

In Figure 76, you see Kendra's Tri-Annual Assessment Summary form, with all data for the year, and in Figure 77, you see the reading graph for Independent-level reading that her school will use to visually document her progress. (They can elect to record either Independent reading level, Instructional reading level, or both. In this district, the Independent reading level has been selected.)

These records document a year of learning for this young student. She progressed from processing texts at level C, with only a few lines of print, many easy high-frequency words, and very simple stories, to fluent reading of texts at level J, with more complex plots, challenging content, and many demands on her word solving abilities. Her teacher noted Kendra's increase in fluency and phrasing; she has built a complex reading process. Although Kendra could read level K at high accuracy, her recommended placement level for beginning grade two was J or K. Kendra will continue to need strong instruction in comprehension and in fluency and phrasing.

Kendra's September Assessment Conference

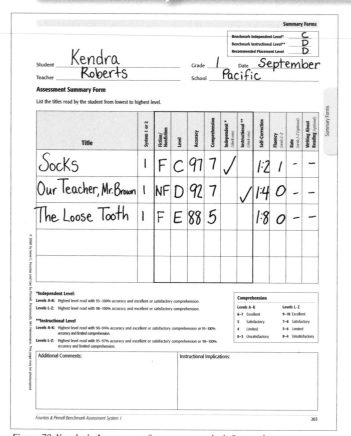

Figure 70. Kendra's Assessment Summary, grade 1, September

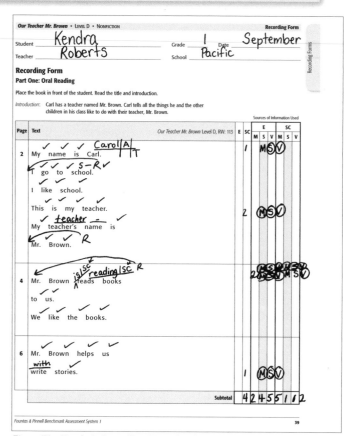

Figure 71a. Kendra's Recording Form, level D, September

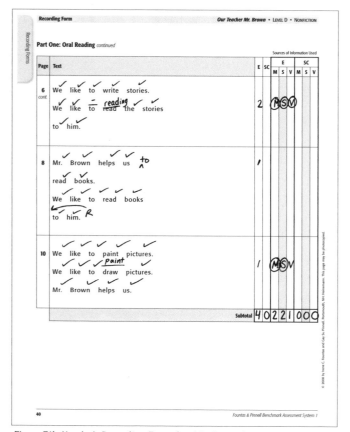

Figure 71b. Kendra's Recording Form, level D, September

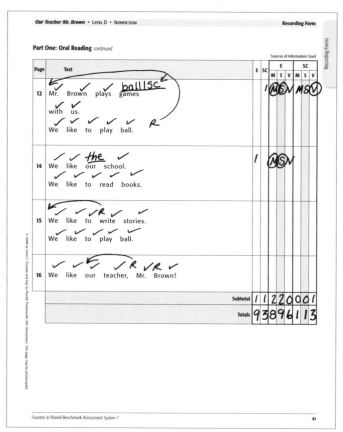

Figure 71c. Kendra's Recording Form, level D, September

Kendra's September Assessment Conference (*continued*)

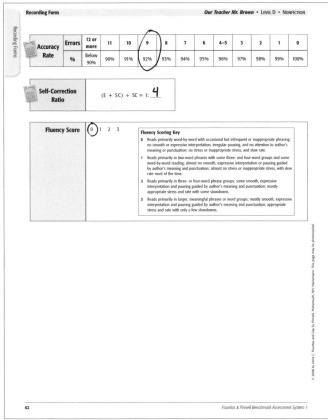

Figure 71d. Kendra's Recording Form, level D, September

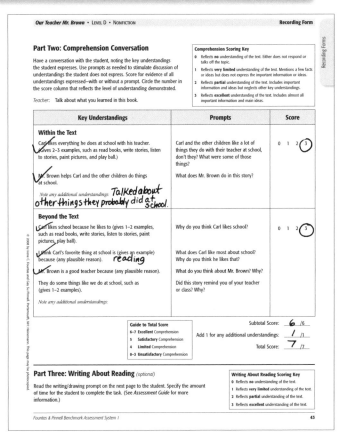

Figure 71e. Kendra's Recording Form, level D, September

Kendra's January Assessment Conference

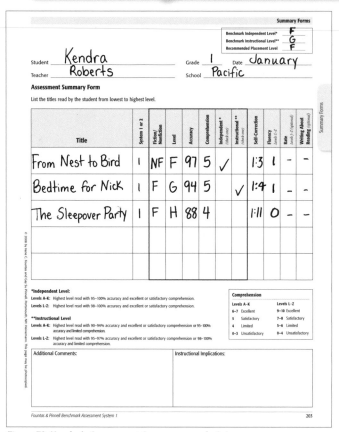

Figure 72. Kendra's Assessment Summary, grade 1, January

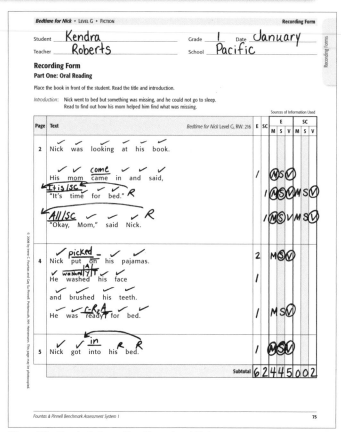

Figure 73a. Kendra's Recording Form, level G, January

Figure 73b. Kendra's Recording Form, level G, January

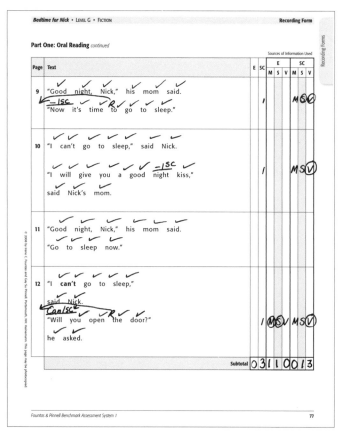

Figure 73c. Kendra's Recording Form, level G, January

Kendra's January Assessment Conference *(continued)*

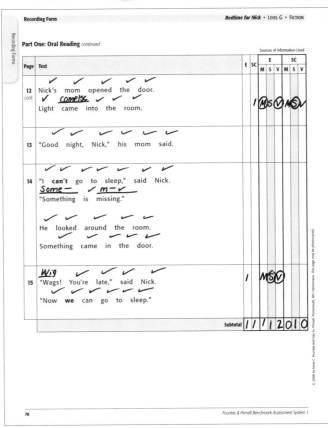

Figure 73d. Kendra's Recording Form, level G, January

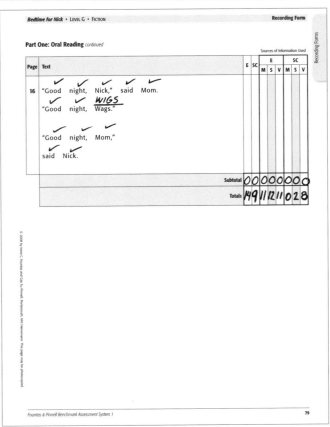

Figure 73e. Kendra's Recording Form, level G, January

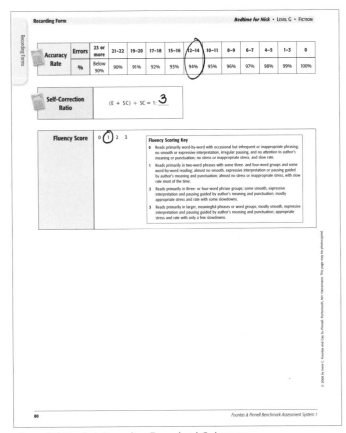

Figure 73f. Kendra's Recording Form, level G, January

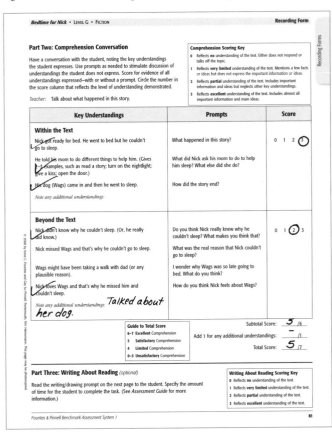

Figure 73g. Kendra's Recording Form, level G, January

Kendra's June Assessment Conference

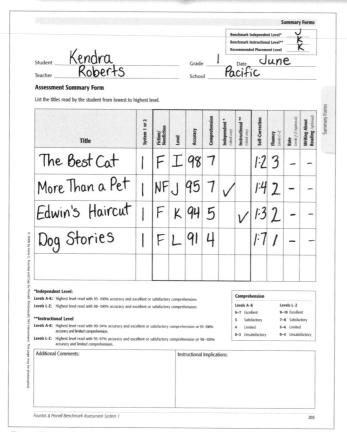

Figure 74. Kendra's Assessment Summary, grade 1, June

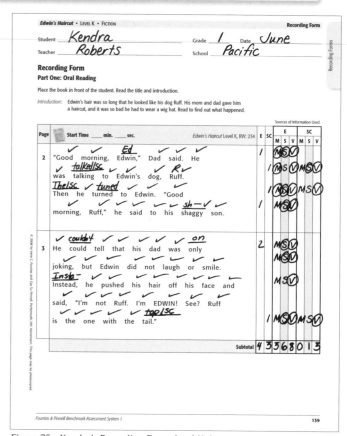

Figure 75a. Kendra's Recording Form, level K, June

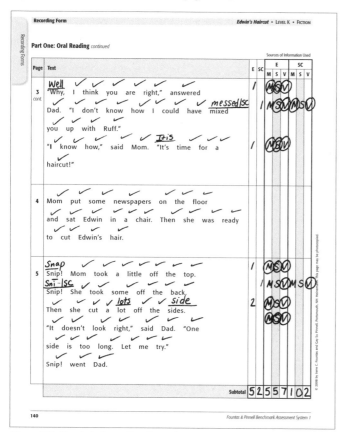

Figure 75b. Kendra's Recording Form, level K, June

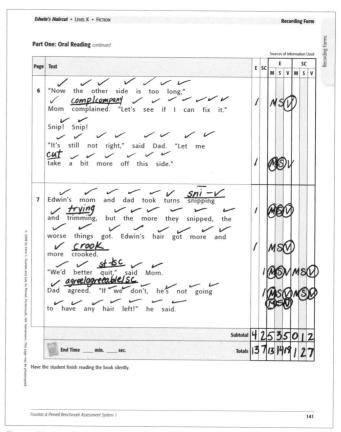

Figure 75c. Kendra's Recording Form, level K, June

Kendra's June Assessment Conference *(continued)*

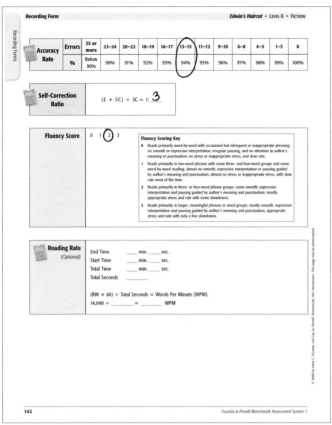

Figure 75d. Kendra's Recording Form, level K, June

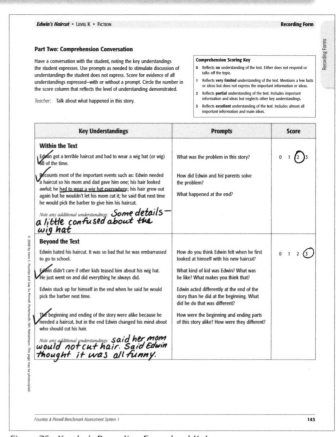

Figure 75e. Kendra's Recording Form, level K, June

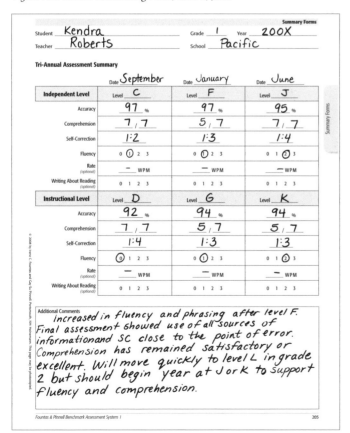

Figure 76. Kendra's Tri-Annual Assessment Summary, grade 1

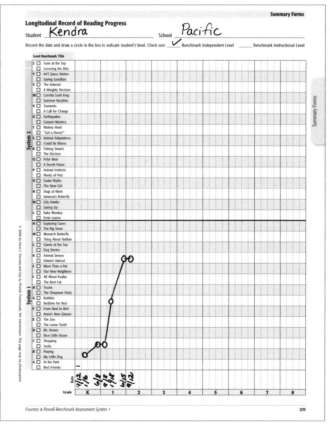

Figure 77. Kendra's Longitudinal Record of Reading Progress

Professional Development Options

Now that you have read about the Fountas & Pinnell Benchmark Assessment System, you can further enhance your learning in a variety of ways. In your kit are critical tools for extending your professional knowledge and skill in assessment, both in this *Assessment Guide* and on the accompanying *Professional Development* DVD. The DVD offers many features to help you learn how to administer the Benchmark Assessment from beginning to end. Tutorials with practice sessions allow you to try your hand at coding specific reading behaviors after viewing model demonstrations. Examples of oral readings and comprehension conversations at different levels can help to build knowledge and broaden your experience as you practice your assessment skills. (Using the DVD with colleagues is a good way to assure that all the teachers in your building are working with consistent guidelines.) You can also log onto the fountasandpinnellbenchmarkassessment.com website to learn about in-person seminars at your school or district as well as to get ongoing information and updates related to your Fountas & Pinnell Benchmark Assessment System.

Appendices

Appendix A contains detailed descriptions of critical features in the Benchmark books.

Appendix B contains a brief description and table of contents for the *Benchmark Assessment Forms* book and CD-ROM.

Appendix C describes the *Data Management* CD-ROM.

Appendix D describes the *Professional Development* DVD

Frequently Asked Questions

Glossary

Appendix A: Benchmark Books

Benchmark books are the centerpiece of the Benchmark Assessment System. They provide the material for the student's oral reading from which the teacher observes many dimensions of reading behavior. In System 1, there are twenty-eight books, fourteen fiction and fourteen nonfiction, ranging from the easiest level, A, to the hardest level, N. There is one fiction and one nonfiction book at each level.

Each fiction and nonfiction book has been written and edited to represent the designated Fountas and Pinnell level. Each represents the specific characteristics of that level. You can find very detailed analyses of texts at each level of the gradient, A–Z, in *Leveled Books for Readers, K–8: Matching Texts to Readers*

for Effective Teaching (Heinemann, 2006) and *The Continuum of Literacy Learning: A Guide for Teaching K–8* (Heinemann, 2008).

In this section, we briefly describe the twenty-eight benchmark books. If you look at the lists in bullets, you will see some important descriptions of each book. These characteristics emerged from analyzing the text to place it on the gradient. They are descriptions of what makes the book easier or harder and are related to the demands the text makes of the reader. Reading these descriptions will help you realize what the reader has to do to read the book. If the reader is successful, then you have good evidence that he or she can meet the demands of texts on the level.

We like to slide.

10   11

Best Friends

Fiction level A
Total words: 32

Two girls tell all the things they like to do together.

Features of this text are:

- ▶ one four-word sentence on every other page

- ▶ clear spaces between words

- ▶ print in large font on the left side of the page layout

- ▶ simple illustrations that provide a clear clue to the meaning of the print

- ▶ easy high-frequency words

- ▶ familiar topic

I can jump.

At the Park

Nonfiction level A

Total words: 24

A boy and his dad have fun together at the park.

Features of this text are:

> ▶ one three-word sentence on every other page
>
> ▶ print in large font in white space on the left side of the page layout
>
> ▶ simple illustrations that provide a clear clue to the meaning of the print
>
> ▶ easy high-frequency words
>
> ▶ familiar topic

My Little Dog

Fiction level B

Total words: 55

A little girl tells all the things her little dog likes to do with her.

Features of this text are:

▶ two lines of print on each page—alternating picture and print pages

▶ print on the left in a large font with clear spaces between words

▶ simple illustrations that provide a clear clue to the meaning of the print

▶ easy high-frequency words

▶ familiar topic

I like to play
with the ball.

Playing

Nonfiction level B
Total words: 56

A little girl tells all of the things she likes to play with.

Features of this text are:

- ▶ two lines of print on each page—alternating print and picture pages
- ▶ print on the left in a large font with clear spaces between words
- ▶ simple illustrations that provide a clear clue to the meaning of the print
- ▶ easy high-frequency words
- ▶ repeating language structures
- ▶ repeating pattern but varying *the*, *my*, and *a*
- ▶ familiar topic

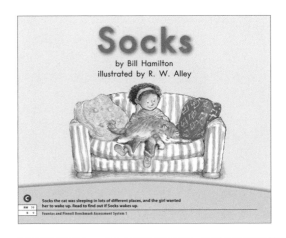

Socks was sleeping
on my chair.
I said,
"Wake up, Socks!"

4   5

Socks

Fiction level C
Total words: 79

A girl tries to wake up her cat, Socks, and finally succeeds.

Features of this text are:

- ▶ four lines of print on each page—alternating print and picture pages

- ▶ each new sentence starting on the left margin

- ▶ print on the left in a large font with clear spaces between words

- ▶ line breaks that suggest phrasing

- ▶ simple dialogue, signaled by *said* and quotation marks

- ▶ two alternative structures for dialogue

- ▶ repetition of language structures

- ▶ easy high-frequency words

- ▶ narrative with problem, events, and solution

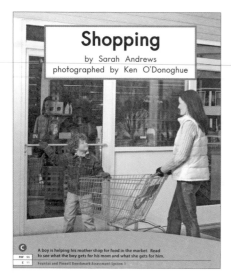  

"Get some carrots,"
Mom said.
10

I put the carrots
in the cart.
11

Shopping

Nonfiction level C
Total words: 96

A boy and his mother are shopping for food in the market. The mother does the directing until the last page, when the boy gets a reward.

Features of this text are:

- ▶ two lines of print at the bottom of every page
- ▶ each new sentence starting on the left margin
- ▶ large font with clear spaces between words
- ▶ line breaks that suggest phrasing
- ▶ simple dialogue in a consistent structure throughout the book and with speakers
- ▶ told in first person
- ▶ repetition of language structures
- ▶ easy high-frequency words and names for food

The Nice Little House

Fiction level D
Total words: 129

Animals go into a little house, and all of them say, "What a nice little house!" But things change when a skunk enters the little house. To the skunk, the now empty house is a "nice big house."

Features of this text are:

- ▶ varying number of lines of print
- ▶ large font with clear spaces between words
- ▶ line breaks that suggest phrasing
- ▶ each new sentence starting on the left margin
- ▶ dialogue
- ▶ word in bold to indicate stress
- ▶ repetition of language structures
- ▶ twist of plot at the end

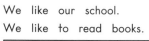

We like our school.
We like to read books.

We like to write stories.
We like to play ball.

14

15

Our Teacher Mr. Brown

Nonfiction level D
Total words: 113

Carl has a teacher named Mr. Brown. Carl tells all of the things he and the other children like to do with their teacher.

Features of this text are:

▶ varying number of lines on pages

▶ large font with clear spaces between words

▶ familiar topics

▶ line breaks that suggest phrasing

▶ each new sentence starting on the left margin

▶ clear photographs to show actions described in the text

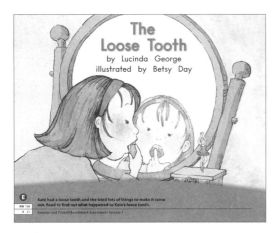

Kate played
with her tooth
at lunch.
She wiggled it
and wiggled it.

10

"Don't wiggle your tooth,"
said Ben.
"I want to eat my lunch."

11

The Loose Tooth

Fiction level E
Total words: 198

Kate has a loose tooth and she tries lots of things to make it come out. Nothing
works until the end when she gets the idea of eating an apple.

Features of this text are:

▸ varying number of lines on each page

▸ prepositional phrases that make sentences more complex

▸ more variety in vocabulary

▸ dialogue that is divided by speaker identification

▸ four different speakers

▸ line breaks that suggest phrasing

▸ each new sentence starting on the left margin

▸ narrative with a problem, events, and a solution

The Zoo

Nonfiction level E
Total words: 137

Each page tells about a different animal at the zoo, with the last page showing the entrance to the zoo itself.

Features of this text are:

- ▶ varying number of lines of print but at least four on every page
- ▶ print on left pages, with photographs of animals on right pages
- ▶ interesting facts about the animal included on every page layout
- ▶ only one repeating language structure, with the rest of the text not patterned
- ▶ line breaks that suggest phrasing
- ▶ each new sentence starting on the left margin
- ▶ information in categories

Anna and her mom walked
to school.

Anna looked at her new teacher.
She opened her backpack and
put on her new glasses.

Anna's New Glasses

Fiction level F
Total words: 220

Anna is getting ready for school, and her mom says she might need to get glasses to see. Anna doesn't want to wear her glasses until she sees that her new teacher has a pair just like them.

Features of this text are:

- ▸ varying lines of print on each page
- ▸ line breaks that suggest phrasing
- ▸ dialogue with a variety of structures, including divided dialogue
- ▸ three speakers
- ▸ each new sentence starting on the left margin
- ▸ words in bold to suggest stress
- ▸ narrative with a problem, plot development, and resolution

From Nest to Bird

Nonfiction level F
Total words: 165

A mother bird makes a nest with sticks and grass and then lays her eggs in the nest. The text describes the mother bird as she keeps the eggs warm and feeds the baby birds once they hatch. The text ends with the baby birds learning to fly.

Features of this text are:

▶ varying lines of print

▶ language that is not repetitive

▶ simple declarative sentences, but longer than previous levels

▶ question-and-answer format

▶ line breaks that suggest phrasing

▶ each new sentence starting on the left margin

▶ writer speaking directly to the reader

▶ simple factual material in chronological sequence

Nick put on his pajamas.
He washed his face
and brushed his teeth.
He was ready for bed.

Nick got into his bed.

4

5

Bedtime for Nick

Fiction level G
Total words: 216

Nick goes to bed but something is missing and he cannot go to sleep.
The "something" turns out to be his dog Wags.

Features of this text are:

▶ varying lines of print

▶ dialogue between two speakers in a variety of
structures, including divided dialogue

▶ line breaks and words in bold to suggest phrasing and word stress

▶ each new sentence starting on the left margin

▶ narrative with a problem and solution

▶ simple mystery inviting the reader to guess what is missing

What is inside all the bubbles?
Bubbles are like little balloons.
They are filled with air.

6 | 7

Bubbles

Nonfiction level G
Total words: 152

This informational text provides factual material about all kinds of bubbles. Readers learn that bubbles are filled with air. It ends with something familiar— bubble gum. The gum pops on the last page.

Features of this text are:

- ▶ varying lines of print on the page

- ▶ large font with clear space between words

- ▶ information presented in logical sequence

- ▶ each new sentence starting on the left margin

- ▶ one sentence breaking over the last two pages

- ▶ readers asked to take a closer look at something familiar

The Sleepover Party

Fiction level H
Total words: 288

Jim is invited to his first sleepover party. He is a little worried about being away from home overnight, and also he isn't sure whether he should take his stuffed dog Mugsy. He leaves the toy at home, but in the end, Mugsy comes to the party after all.

Features of this text are:

- ▶ varying lines of text
- ▶ line breaks that suggest phrasing
- ▶ each new sentence starting on the left margin
- ▶ expressions, such as "after all"
- ▶ dialogue among six speakers in a variety of structures
- ▶ a range of easy high-frequency words
- ▶ narrative with a problem and solution
- ▶ surprise ending

This is a fire truck.
Fire trucks help put out fires.
This truck has a long hose
that shoots water on the fire.

4

Trucks

Nonfiction level H
Total words: 188

This text presents information about six different kinds of trucks. The focus is on the function of the truck to do different jobs.

Features of this text are:

▸ four to seven lines of print on the left pages

▸ clear pictures of trucks doing their jobs on the right pages

▸ variety in language structures; no repetitive structures

▸ each new sentence starting on the left margin

▸ a range of easy high-frequency words

▸ information presented in categories

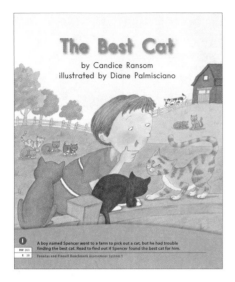

The Best Cat

Fiction level I
Total words: 334

A boy named Spencer goes to a farm to pick out a cat, but he has trouble finding the best cat for him. The illustrations show a tiny kitten following Spencer as he approaches cat after cat. In the end, the kitten finds him, and Spencer decides it is the best cat of all.

Features of this text are:

▶ most pages with six or seven lines of print and print on every page

▶ large font with clear spaces between words

▶ variety of high-frequency words

▶ dialogue in a variety of structures

▶ line breaks that mark phrases

▶ use of bold to suggest which words to stress

▶ each new sentence starting on the left margin

▶ narrative with a problem and solution

▶ illustrations that enhance meaning and lead the reader to predict the ending

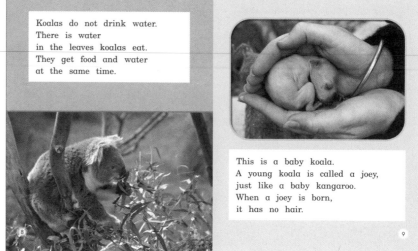

All About Koalas

Nonfiction level I
Total words: 217

This informational text presents many interesting facts about koalas, including where they live, what they look like, and what they eat. Readers will learn about baby koalas, called *joeys*, and how they grow. They will also read about the problems koalas face because of logging.

Features of this text are:

- three to five lines of print on most pages
- photographs on each page that illustrate the meaning of the print
- some technical vocabulary (*koala, joey, pouch*)
- information presented in categories
- each new sentence starting on the left margin
- very simple presentation of an environmental problem

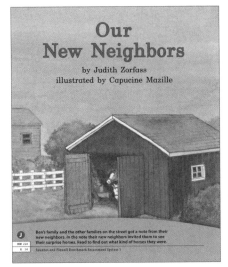

"Horses?" Everyone looked at one another.

"Horses on our street?" asked Dad.

"I hope they're ponies," said Ben. "When we have birthday parties, we can have pony rides."

"I hope they're big white horses," said Polly. "Maybe they'll give us a ride."

Our New Neighbors

Fiction level J
Total words: 428

Ben's family and the other families on his street get an invitation from their new neighbors, Max and Flo. The new neighbors invite them to see their surprise horses, and everyone imagines what those horses might be like. Right before the last page, there are some "clues" that may help readers to predict the ending—that the horses are on a carousel.

Features of this text are:

▶ varied number of lines of print on each page

▶ paragraphs indicated by space between lines

▶ new sentences starting after ending punctuation within lines

▶ a variety of dialogue among multiple speakers

▶ "thought bubbles" with pictures to show inner thoughts of characters

▶ a simple mystery with "clues" that allow the reader to predict

▶ narrative with problem and solution

More Than a Pet

Nonfiction level J
Total words: 319

This informational text presents two kinds of dogs that are "more than pets" because of the services they give people. Therapy dogs help people feel better, and service dogs help them to do things.

Features of this text are:

▶ varied number of lines of print on each page

▶ words in bold to indicate concepts

▶ some technical words (*therapy, service, harness*)

▶ paragraphs indicated by space between lines

▶ photographs showing dogs performing services

▶ headings to show categories of information

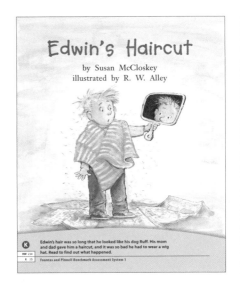

Edwin's Haircut

Fiction level K

Total words: 480

Edwin's hair is so long that he looks like his dog Ruff. His mom and dad give him a haircut that is so bad he has to wear a hat that looks like a wig everywhere. By the end of the story, Edwin is shaggy again, but he makes a decision about who will cut his hair the next time.

Features of this text are:

- four to eight lines of print on most pages
- paragraphs indicated by indentation
- new sentences starting after ending punctuation within lines
- a variety of dialogue among multiple speakers
- "speech bubbles" with words to show inner thoughts of characters
- story carried by dialogue and description of the action
- words to show passage of time ("for a long time," "one morning")
- complex sentences with embedded clauses
- words in all capital letters to show stress
- narrative with a circular plot and satisfying ending

Surprising Animal Senses

Nonfiction level K

Total words: 503

This informational text describes the five senses by comparing people and animals that smell, hear, taste, see, and feel with different parts of their bodies. Two pages present the "super senses" of eagles, bloodhounds, and bats.

Features of this text are:

▶ some full pages of print

▶ use of compare and contrast to present information

▶ question-and-answer format on some pages

▶ new sentences starting after ending punctuation within lines

▶ headings and subheadings to organize and present information

▶ information under the photographs

▶ close-ups in the photographs

▶ table of contents

▶ a summary at the end

Dog Stories

Fiction level L
Total words: 482

April reads a story to her dog Golden Boy. She decides to write a letter to her favorite author, Julia Reed, to ask her to write a book about Golden Boy. When the author writes back, April realizes that you have to write about a dog that you know. She decides to write a book about Golden Boy herself.

Features of this text are:

- ▷ varied number of lines of print on each page

- ▷ pictures and print on every page

- ▷ paragraphs indicated by indentation

- ▷ new sentences starting after ending punctuation within lines

- ▷ a variety of dialogue among two speakers

- ▷ story carried by dialogue and description of the action

- ▷ words to show passage of time ("the next day," "every day")

- ▷ complex sentences with embedded clauses

- ▷ narrative with problem and resolution

- ▷ different genres of text (fiction books, letters) embedded within the narrative

Whale Sounds

Whales communicate with one another. They let each other know where to find food.

Whales make many different sounds. Some whales whistle, cry, or scream. Some burp or chirp. Other whales click. Some whales sound like they are singing. Their songs can last up to 20 minutes.

Whales swim together in groups called *pods*.

12

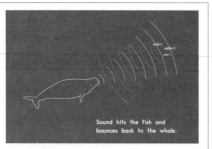

Sound hits the fish and bounces back to the whale.

Some whales use sound to find their way through dark seas. A whale sends out sounds that travel through the water. The sounds bounce off fish, rocks, and other objects.

13

Giants of the Sea

Nonfiction level L
Total words: 436

This informational text provides interesting facts about whales—for example, what they look like, how they live, how they are born, and how they communicate. Facts are extended through graphics that illustrate the whale's size compared to other animals.

Features of this text are:

- four to six lines of print on most pages
- photographs and print on each page
- graphics, including legends under pictures and diagrams with callouts
- headings for sections
- use of compare and contrast to present information
- use of temporal sequence to present information
- some technical vocabulary (*blowholes, blow, calf, pods*)
- new sentences that start after ending punctuation within lines
- paragraphs indicated by space between lines
- headings and subheadings to organize and present information
- table of contents
- glossary

"My little brother drives me crazy," said Hanna. "He is so messy! Nathan doesn't eat food. He wears it. And you wouldn't believe his room!" Hanna rolled her eyes. "It looks like a herd of cattle lives there."

"My brother is a neat freak," said Jerry. "William puts all his stuff away on a shelf in his room, with everything in perfect order, like the books in the library. And you'd better not touch anything."

The Thing About Nathan

Fiction level M
Total words: 624

In this story, a girl named Hanna is tired of her messy younger brother, Nathan. She trades him for a day with her friend Jerry's little brother, William, the "neat freak." After a few hours with William, Hanna learns to appreciate Nathan.

Features of this text are:

- ▷ five to thirteen lines of print on most pages

- ▷ pictures and print on every page

- ▷ paragraphs indicated by indentation

- ▷ words in all capital letters to show stress

- ▷ new sentences that start after ending punctuation within lines

- ▷ a variety of dialogue between two speakers at a time

- ▷ story carried by dialogue and description of the action

- ▷ words and pictures in thought bubbles to show characters' inner dialogue

- ▷ complex sentences with embedded clauses

- ▷ narrative with problem and resolution

- ▷ use of comparison to show character traits

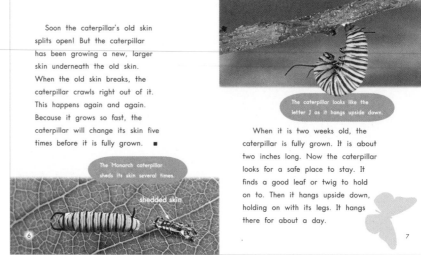

The Life of a Monarch Butterfly

Nonfiction level M
Total words: 512

In this informational text, readers will learn how a monarch butterfly changes from an egg to a caterpillar.

Features of this text are:

▶ eight to ten lines of print on most pages

▶ photographs and print on each page

▶ life cycle diagram with labels

▶ legends and labels with pictures

▶ use of temporal sequence to present information

▶ headings for sections

▶ some technical vocabulary (*chrysalis*)

▶ new sentences starting after ending punctuation within lines

▶ paragraphs indicated by indentation

▶ table of contents

▶ glossary

With five minutes left in the school day, not a single student in room 314 was thinking about school. Outside, snow was falling, piling up like a thick blanket on the street. It was Chicago's first big storm of the year. From Patrick Waite's seat two rows from the window, it looked like six inches had already fallen. The snowflakes were huge and fluffy. Patrick felt dizzy watching them tumble from the sky.

When the bell finally rang, he hurried out the door and down the sidewalk in ankle-deep snow.

"Looks like the number six bus is stuck!" Mr. Henry said.

A stuck bus didn't matter to Patrick. His family's apartment was just five blocks from the school, and he always walked. Patrick grinned. Today, he could pretend he was hiking at the North Pole.

The Big Snow

Fiction level N
Total words: 784

The first big snowstorm of the year causes some problems for Patrick and his family.

Features of this text are:

- ▶ ten to twelve lines of print on most pages

- ▶ smaller font than previous levels

- ▶ many whole pages of print

- ▶ paragraphs indicated by indentation

- ▶ words in all capitals to indicate characters are talking loudly

- ▶ words in italics to indicate stress on words

- ▶ new sentences starting after ending punctuation within lines

- ▶ a variety of dialogue between two speakers at a time

- ▶ story carried by dialogue and description of the action

- ▶ complex sentences with embedded clauses

- ▶ narrative with problem and resolution

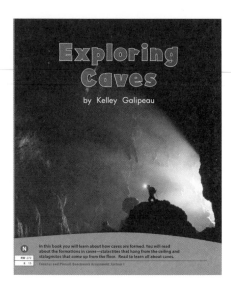

How Are Caves Formed?

Scientists have different ideas about how caves are formed. Most think caves are created by water.

When rain falls, it mixes with an invisible gas in the air. When the water reaches the ground, it seeps into the earth.

The water continues going deeper into the earth until it touches rock. Very slowly, the water eats away at the rock and causes tiny cracks to develop. The cracks in the rock grow wider with time. Then the water flows out and leaves behind a cave.

How Caves Are Formed

1. Rain falls and seeps into the ground.
2. The water goes deeper until it hits rock.
3. The water eats away at the rock, then flows out.
4. A cave remains where the water had been.

Exploring Caves

Nonfiction level N
Total words: 511

In this informational book, readers will learn about how caves are formed. They will read about stalactites and stalagmites, as well as how cavers explore caves safely.

Features of this text are:

- ▶ eight to ten lines of print on most pages
- ▶ photographs and print on each page
- ▶ diagrams with labels
- ▶ legends and labels with pictures
- ▶ use of temporal sequence to present information
- ▶ headings for sections
- ▶ some technical vocabulary (*stalactites, stalagmites, cavers*)
- ▶ key word in italics
- ▶ new sentences that start after ending punctuation within lines
- ▶ paragraphs indicated by indentation
- ▶ table of contents
- ▶ glossary

Appendix B: Assessment Forms Book and CD-ROM

All record-keeping forms for the Fountas & Pinnell Benchmark Assessment System are available in the *Assessment Forms* book as well as in electronic form on the *Assessment Forms* CD-ROM. The following tools are found in both.

Assessment Forms

Recording Forms

The Recording Form is the primary tool for administering the Benchmark Assessment. With it, you observe and code the reader's oral reading behaviors, comprehension conversation, and (optionally) writing or drawing about the reading. There are twenty-eight Recording Forms in *Fountas & Pinnell Benchmark Assessment System 1*, one for each benchmark book.

Summary Forms

1 The Assessment Summary form organizes and displays assessment results from multiple Recording Forms on multiple book readings. The final benchmark levels—Independent, Instructional, and Recommended Placement—as well as additional observations and instructional implications are recorded here.

2 The Bi-annual, Tri-annual, and Quarterly Assessment Summary forms provide three options for tracking student progress across a school year. Choose the one that reflects the number of times in a school year you plan to administer Benchmark Assessments: two (bi-annual), three (tri-annual), or four (quarterly). On this form you record the information from the Assessment Summary form for the Independent and Instructional levels.

3 The Class Record form provides a way for you to see all your students' assessment data in relation to each other. It combines the Independent- and Instructional-level information; the accuracy, comprehension, and fluency scores; and Recommended Placement levels for each child onto a class list. It is useful for determining groups and differentiating instruction.

4 Two Records of Reading Progress give you a picture of progress through the benchmark levels. The Annual Record of Reading Progress is designed for teacher use across one school year. In addition to charting the results of Benchmark Assessments, it may also include interim levels from ongoing running records. The Longitudinal Record of Reading Progress is printed on the student folder as well as in the *Assessment Forms* book and CD-ROM. This progress form can be passed from teacher to teacher over the years of schooling from grade K to middle school to show progress over time.

Optional Assessments

Where-to-Start Word Test

The Where-to-Start Word Test provides a quick way to find a starting place for the text reading assessment. If you do not have sufficient information from the previous teacher or school records or your own observations to judge the starting point for the assessment, this test should save you from having the student read a large number of texts. The Where-to-Start Word Test is a series of lists of increasingly difficult words, organized by grade level. The student's level of performance reading the words predicts the approximate level of text that the student may be able to read.

Reading Interview

The Reading Interview is an optional form that you can use to learn more about a reader's preferences and reading history. It takes about five minutes to administer the interview.

Six Dimensions Fluency Rubric

The Six Dimensions Fluency Rubric provides a detailed way to look at oral reading fluency. It targets five dimensions of fluency—pausing, phrasing, stress, intonation, and rate—and a sixth dimension, integration, which refers to the way the reader orchestrates the other five dimensions. The scale can be used to provide more in-depth evaluation than the simple fluency score on the Fountas & Pinnell Benchmark Assessment System. It can also be used whenever you are observing a reader's behavior, not just during benchmark testing, to assess the aspects of fluency that the reader is demonstrating and those neglected. You can then plan and shape your teaching to do some very specific demonstration and prompting for various aspects of fluency.

Phonics and Word Analysis Assessments

Twenty-two Phonics and Word Analysis Assessments focus on specific reading-processing skills: letter knowledge, early literacy concepts, high-frequency words, phonological awareness, letter-sound relationships, and word structure. Your school or district may want to select an optional assessment that you feel is critical for a particular grade level (such as letter knowledge in kindergarten or P1) as part of the Benchmark Assessment process. Or you may want to diagnose a particular area of learning (such as reading words with vowel clusters) for a child who shows difficulty. If most of your class or a small group is having difficulty in an area (for example, reading two-syllable words), you might want to give them the assessment. In any case, select only assessments that are needed for a particular purpose.

Phonics and Word Analysis Assessments

	Assessment	Category of Learning	Description
1	Letter Recognition	Letter knowledge	Children say the names of the alphabet by recognizing the shapes of uppercase and lowercase letters.
2	Early Literacy Behaviors	Early literacy concepts	Children demonstrate that they know and can use the following conventions related to print: finding specific words within a text; matching words they hear with words they read.
3	Reading High Frequency Words: 25 Words	High frequency words	Children read 25 high frequency words.
4	Reading High Frequency Words: 50 Words	High frequency words	Children read 50 high frequency words.
5	Reading High Frequency Words: 100 Words	High frequency words	Children read 100 high frequency words.
6	Reading High Frequency Words: 200 Words	High frequency words	Children read 200 high frequency words.
7	Phonological Awareness: Initial Sounds	Phonological awareness	Children identify pictures with the same initial sound as a spoken word.
8	Phonological Awareness: Blending Words	Phonological awareness	Children hear and say the individual sounds in a word and then blend the sounds to say the word.
9	Phonological Awareness: Segmenting Words	Phonological awareness	Children say a word and then say the individual sounds separately but in sequence.
10	Phonological Awareness: Rhyming	Phonological awareness	Children match words that sound alike in the ending part (rime).
11	Word Writing	Letter-sound relationships	Children write all of the words they can within a time limit.
12	Writing Picture Names	Letter-sound relationships	Children say words slowly and write the sounds they hear.
13	Phonograms	Spelling patterns	Children read words with simple phonogram patterns.
14	Consonant Blends	Letter-sound relationships	Children say words and identify consonant clusters.

Optional Phonics and Word Analysis Assessments

Continued on next page

Phonics and Word Analysis Assessments, continued		
Assessment	**Category of Learning**	**Description**
15 Vowel Clusters	Letter-sound relationships	Children read words with vowels that appear together and represent one sound.
16 Suffixes	Word structure	Children read words with suffixes that change the part of speech.
17 Compound Words	Word structure	Children read simple compound words and identify the two words that have been put together.
18 One- and Two-syllable Words	Word structure	Children say a word, clap for each syllable, and identify the number of syllables in the word.
19 Syllables in Longer Words	Word structure	Children demonstrate that they can hear syllable breaks, can count the number of syllables in a word, and have a beginning understanding of where to divide a word when hyphenating.
20 Grade 1 Word Features Test	Letter-sound recognition	Children read 30 words, which include a variety of features: consonant sounds, short and long vowel sounds, simple phonogram patterns, consonant clusters and digraphs, double consonants, multisyllable words, compound words.
21 Grade 2 Word Features Test	Letter-sound recognition	Children read 30 words, which include a variety of features: possessives, double vowels, multisyllable words, long vowel sounds, contractions, *y* as a vowel sound, prefixes, consonant clusters, consonant digraphs, double vowels.
22 Grade 3 Word Features Test	Word structure	Children read 30 words, which include a variety of features: phonogram patterns in monosyllabic words, syllable patterns in multisyllable words, consonant digraphs, contractions, prefixes, compound words.

Optional Phonics and Word Analysis Assessments

Vocabulary Assessments

A selection of Vocabulary Assessments focuses on word meaning and evaluates a student's word knowledge (concept words, vocabulary in context), understanding of word relationships (synonyms, antonyms, roots, analogies), and ability to derive the precise meaning of words in the context of a short book (vocabulary in context).

	Name	Category	Description
Benchmark 1			
1	Concept Words: Number	Vocabulary	Prompted by a picture card, children say the related concept word.
2	Concept Words: Color	Vocabulary	Prompted by a picture card, children say the related concept word.
3	Concept Words in Isolation	Vocabulary	Children read and talk about a series of concept words: days of the week, seasons of the year, months of the year, weather words, position words (first, second, third, etc.).
4	Concept Words in Sentences	Vocabulary	Children read sentences that include concept words (number words, days of the week, seasons of the year, months of the year, weather words, etc.), locate the words, and then reread the sentences.
5	Concept Words	Vocabulary	Children read concept words and sort them into appropriate categories.
6	Synonyms I	Vocabulary	Children locate words that mean the same or about the same as words read by the teacher.
7	Synonyms II	Vocabulary	Children read and identify words that mean the same or almost the same thing.
8	Antonyms I	Vocabulary	Children read and identify words that mean the opposite or almost the opposite.
9	Antonyms II	Vocabulary	Children read and identify words that mean the opposite or almost the opposite.

Vocabulary Assessments

Continued on next page

	Name	Category	Description
			Benchmark 1, continued
10	Homophones I	Vocabulary	Children listen to a sentence and circle the word (homophone) that has the right meaning in the sentence.
11	Homophones II	Vocabulary in context	Children read a sentence and write the correct homophone in the blank space.
12	Level A fiction	Vocabulary in context	Children use context to correctly identify the meaning of three words from the book *Best Friends.*
13	Level A nonfiction	Vocabulary in context	Children use context to correctly identify the meaning of three words from the book *At the Park.*
14	Level B fiction	Vocabulary in context	Children use context to correctly identify the meaning of three words from the book *My Little Dog.*
15	Level B nonfiction	Vocabulary in context	Children use context to correctly identify the meaning of three words from the book *Playing.*
16	Level C fiction	Vocabulary in context	Children use context to correctly identify the meaning of three words from the book *Socks.*
17	Level C nonfiction	Vocabulary in context	Children use context to correctly identify the meaning of three words from the book *Shopping.*
18	Level D fiction	Vocabulary in context	Children use context to correctly identify the meaning of four words from the book *The Nice Little House.*
19	Level D nonfiction	Vocabulary in context	Children use context to correctly identify the meaning of four words from the book *Our Teacher Mr. Brown.*
20	Level E fiction	Vocabulary in context	Children use context to correctly identify the meaning of four words from the book *The Loose Tooth.*
21	Level E nonfiction	Vocabulary in context	Children use context to correctly identify the meaning of four words from the book *The Zoo.*
22	Level F fiction	Vocabulary in context	Children use context to correctly identify the meaning of four words from the book *Anna's New Glasses.*
23	Level F nonfiction	Vocabulary in context	Children use context to correctly identify the meaning of four words from the book *From Nest to Bird.*
24	Level G fiction	Vocabulary in context	Children use context to correctly identify the meaning of four words from the book *Bedtime for Nick.*

Vocabulary Assessments

Continued on next page

	Name	Category	Description
			Benchmark 1, continued
25	Level G nonfiction	Vocabulary in context	Children use context to correctly identify the meaning of four words from the book *Bubbles*.
26	Level H fiction	Vocabulary in context	Children use context to correctly identify the meaning of five words from the book *The Sleepover Party*.
27	Level H nonfiction	Vocabulary in context	Children use context to correctly identify the meaning of five words from the book *Trucks*.
28	Level I fiction	Vocabulary in context	Children use context to correctly identify the meaning of five words from the book *The Best Cat*.
29	Level I nonfiction	Vocabulary in context	Children use context to correctly identify the meaning of five words from the book *All About Koalas*.
30	Level J fiction	Vocabulary in context	Children use context to correctly identify the meaning of five words from the book *Our New Neighbors*.
31	Level J nonfiction	Vocabulary in context	Children use context to correctly identify the meaning of five words from the book *More Than a Pet*.
32	Level K fiction	Vocabulary in context	Children use context to correctly identify the meaning of five words from the book *Edwin's Haircut*.
33	Level K nonfiction	Vocabulary in context	Children use context to correctly identify the meaning of five words from the book *Surprising Animal Senses*.
34	Level L fiction	Vocabulary in context	Children use context to correctly identify the meaning of five words from the book *Dog Stories*.
35	Level L nonfiction	Vocabulary in context	Children use context to correctly identify the meaning of five words from the book *Giants of the Sea*.
36	Level M fiction	Vocabulary in context	Children use context to correctly identify the meaning of five words from the book *The Thing About Nathan*.
37	Level M nonfiction	Vocabulary in context	Children use context to correctly identify the meaning of five words from the book *The Life of a Monarch Butterfly*.
38	Level N fiction	Vocabulary in context	Children use context to correctly identify the meaning of five words from the book *The Big Snow*.
39	Level N nonfiction	Vocabulary in context	Children use context to correctly identify the meaning of five words from the book *Exploring Caves*.

Vocabulary Assessments

Resources

Each of these charts summarizes a key Benchmark Assessment procedure.

▶ Assessment at-a-Glance provides a reference for the assessment conference.

▶ Coding and Scoring Errors at-a-Glance describes the coding and scoring errors and self-corrections in an oral reading evaluation.

▶ Scoring and Analyzing at-a-Glance summarizes how to make the final calculations and observations.

▶ Guide for Observing and Noting Reading Behaviors lists questions to help you analyze ways a reader is processing text.

▶ The Text Gradient correlates Fountas and Pinnell levels with grade levels.

▶ Finding Easy, Instructional, and Hard Texts is a quick reference for selecting the right benchmark books during an assessment conference.

Assessment Forms Book and CD-ROM

All of the assessment forms are available either in reproducible form in the *Assessment Forms* book or as printable PDF files on the *Assessment Forms* CD-ROM. On the CD-ROM, you can navigate to different tabs for Recording Forms, Summary Forms, Optional Assessments, and Resources. Then you can select which forms you want, view the files in Adobe Acrobat Reader, and print them as you wish.

You can select, view, and print Recording Forms by level, title, or genre. You can also print them with enlarged book text for easier reading and coding. Summary forms for a single assessment conference and forms for tracking a student's progress are also readily accessible.

The three parts of the optional assessments can be viewed and printed from the CD-ROM, either separately or together. To help you make decisions about which optional assessments to administer, you can also view and print the entire list to use as a reference.

The fourth tab offers the following resources:

▶ Assessment at-a-Glance

▶ Coding Errors

▶ Coding and Scoring at-a-Glance

▶ Scoring and Analyzing at-a-Glance

▶ Guide for Observing and Noting Reading Behaviors

▶ Text Gradient

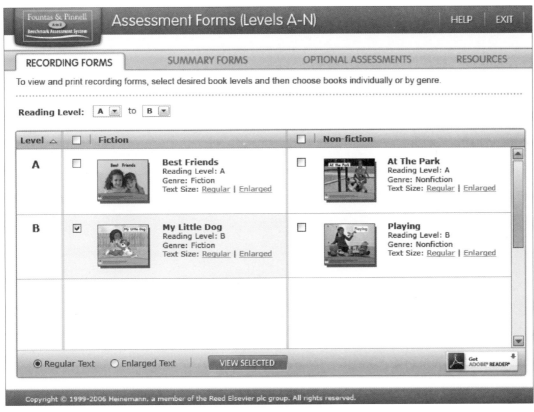

Recording Forms can be viewed and printed from the CD-ROM.

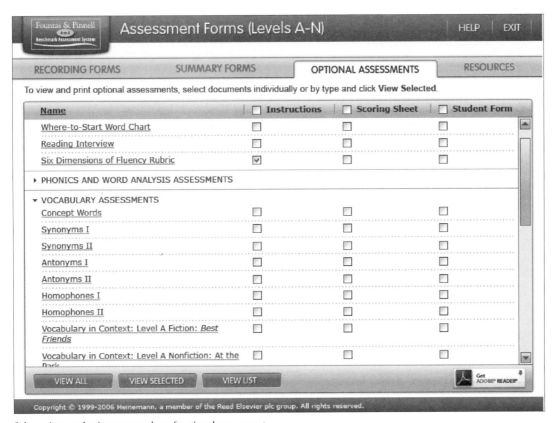

Select, view, and print any number of optional assessments.

Appendix C:
Data Management CD-ROM

The *Data Management* CD-ROM allows you to track and analyze assessment data for individual students and entire classes. Once you have logged in, you can create a class and enter student data, either manually or by importing it from another file.

After administering the assessments, you can enter assessment data from individual recording forms and/or the assessment summary forms. You can view an individual student's assessment summary for any administration period.

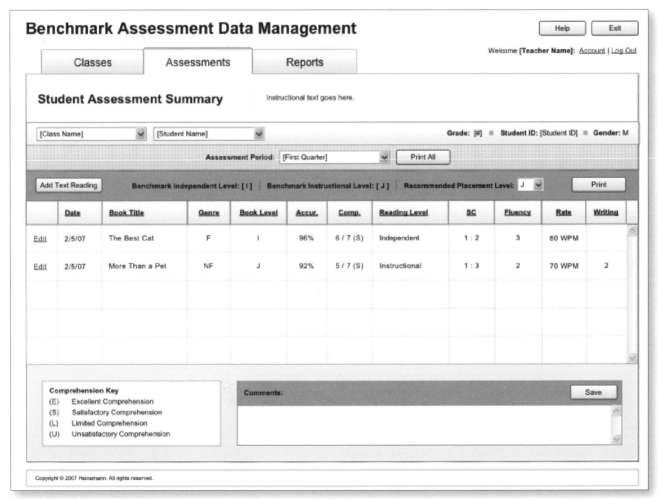

Individual student assessment summary

You can view a class assessment summary, including all students' benchmark levels and associated data. Class assessment summaries can also be printed by assessment administration period. To facilitate data analysis, records can be sorted by any data category. For example, to help you form instructional groups, student records can be sorted by Benchmark Instructional level.

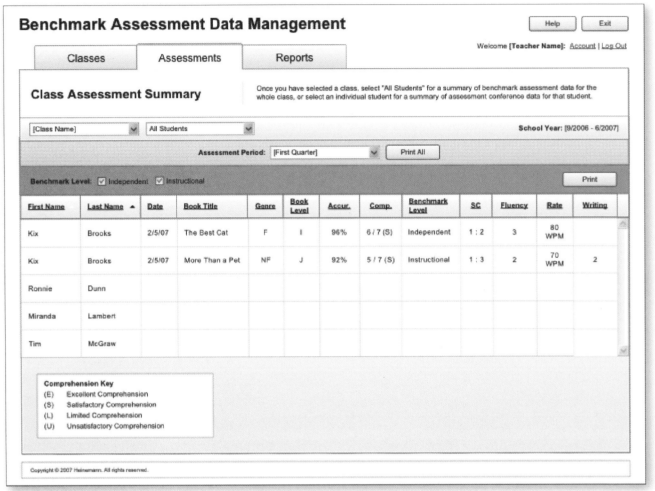

Class assessment summary

A variety of graphing options allow you to analyze assessment data to identify patterns and track progress over time. For example, you can create a report that graphs an individual student's Benchmark Instructional reading levels at several points in the school year.

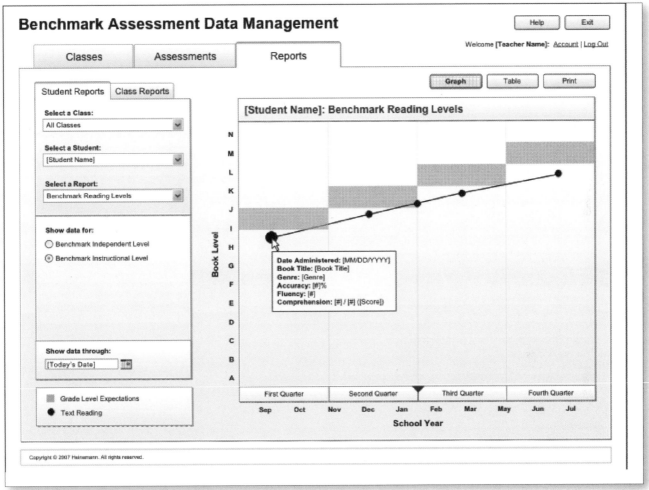

Individual student progress report showing benchmark levels for the school year

You can also graph benchmark levels or comprehension scores for an entire class to get a picture of overall performance. In order to inform instruction, teachers can use reports to reflect on student data patterns. For example, if your class reports show that students generally have high scores for "within the text" comprehension, but low scores for "beyond the text" comprehension, you might plan to focus subsequent instruction on making inferences and other interpretive skills. Printed reports allow teachers to convey periodic progress to students, parents, and administrators.

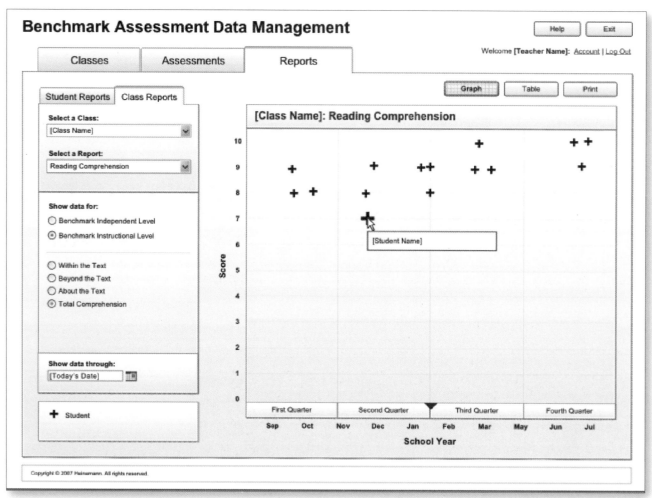

Class progress report indicating total comprehension scores for an entire class

Appendix D: Professional Development DVD

The *Professional Development* DVD allows teachers to view a variety of assessments in action. Its modular design offers teachers the opportunity to learn about each component of the benchmark assessment with varying degrees of guidance, depending on individual needs.

The *Professional Development* DVD provides the following options for learning about the Fountas and Pinnell Benchmark Assessment System:

▶ a general overview of the benchmark assessment system and its components

▶ explanations of each step in the benchmark assessment procedure, including preparation, book selection, oral readings,

comprehension conversations, and optional student writing, as well as coding, scoring, analyzing, and interpreting an assessment

▶ guided tutorials that offer practice in coding oral reading behaviors

▶ instruction about scoring and analyzing oral reading behaviors, fluency, and comprehension, with authentic examples of student readings and comprehension conversations for demonstration and practice

▶ teacher reflections on benchmark assessments, considering their instructional implications for particular students

▶ a chance to practice applying new knowledge and skills while viewing a sample assessment conference from beginning to end

Kulsum reads *Bubbles* while Stephanie assesses her.

Frequently Asked Questions

General

What does the term *level* mean?

A level refers to the difficulty of the book in relation to other books placed along a continuum from A to Z, easiest to hardest. We examine the characteristics of a book and place it along a gradient of books in relation to each other. A level designates the books as easier than the level after (later in the alphabet) and harder than the level before it (earlier in the alphabet). We use ten characteristics to determine a level and the composite of characteristics contributes to its final designation. For a detailed explanation of each level, see *Leveled Books, K–8: Matching Texts to Readers for Effective Teaching* (Heinemann, 2006).

Do the Fountas & Pinnell Benchmark levels match the guided reading levels?

Yes. This assessment is specifically designed to match the guided reading levels described in *Leveled Books, K–8: Matching Texts to Readers for Effective Teaching* (Heinemann, 2006) and other publications by Fountas and Pinnell.

How can I use this benchmark system to match books leveled with other systems?

The website fountasandpinnellleveledbooks.com lists over 25,000 books leveled using the Fountas and Pinnell system, and the site is updated every month. Also, many publishers place several different kinds of levels on books and/or offer correlation charts. But you can also use the benchmark texts as models or prototypes

to help you level other books. Then you can test your leveled books with students. Remember that in Benchmark 2, the texts are necessarily shorter than most of the texts students read.

Should I assess both fiction and nonfiction reading?

The fiction and nonfiction book at each level are equivalent measures. You can use either text to determine the child's ability to read at that level.

How long does it take to administer the assessment to a student?

At the earliest levels it may take fifteen or twenty minutes while it may take about thirty or forty minutes when your students are reading the longer texts and the discussions are more substantive. In this guide we make several suggestions on how to be efficient with your use of time.

How often should you administer the Benchmark Assessment?

We suggest that you administer the assessment at the beginning of the year to know where to start the teaching with each student. You may want to conduct the assessment in the middle of the year to take stock of student progress, though you may already have the information from your ongoing use of running records or reading records in instruction. At the end of the year you may want to make a final record of the student's growth across the year.

Are Benchmark Assessment books ones the students may have read before?

In the Benchmark Assessment the students are reading an unseen text, or a text that the student has not read before. You can expect the text to be a little harder than it would be if they have read it once before.

Is the Fountas & Pinnell Benchmark Assessment System a standardized test?

Yes, it is a standardized assessment. The administration, coding, scoring, and interpretation are standardized in procedures to get reliable results. We expect that once you get the standardized results, you will review the data to make good judgments for instruction. Good teacher decisions based on data are essential.

Is Benchmark Assessment authentic assessment?

You cannot get closer to authentic assessment than with the Fountas & Pinnell Benchmark Assessment System. The student reads several books, thinks and talks about them, and writes about reading. This is not only a valid assessment of the competencies you want to measure, but is a good use of teacher and student time!

Some teachers feel that the assessment is an accountability measure for them. Do you agree?

As teachers, we need to seek information about our students as well as information that informs us about how our teaching is impacting their learning. At the beginning of the year, the assessment gives information about the starting points of the learners. As the school year progresses, the assessment becomes a tool for measuring the growth of the students and the effectiveness of your teaching. The series of assessments conducted over several years will reflect the success of the entire school in bringing each child forward in literacy outcomes.

How does this Benchmark Assessment package help me with my leveled book program?

The Fountas & Pinnell Benchmark Assessment is designed to help you collect reliable evidence of student competencies and reading levels so you can begin your teaching where the learners are—at the optimal instructional level and with in-depth knowledge of his reading behaviors—bringing each reader forward in his competencies. No other assessment has been directly linked to the Fountas and Pinnell levels to date, so you will also have a reliable and valid assessment to link to guided reading small-group reading instruction.

How does the Benchmark Assessment support my ability to conduct the assessment conference with students whose first language is not English?

You will notice that in the Assessment Guide we have provided specific support to help you understand how language differences should be noticed in the administration and interpretation of the assessment. In addition, case examples of English language learners describe and comment on real situations for you to think about and learn from.

How does the Fountas and Pinnell Benchmark Assessment contribute to my knowledge of students and how they develop as readers?

You will find that the comprehensive assessment procedures and the variety of tools and options provided in the Benchmark Assessment package are rich resources for helping you systematically examine a student's strengths and needs and begin to think about the important link between assessment and instruction. You will find detailed information about analyzing the reading behaviors of the student and linking them to specific instructional goals in the Assessment Guide. The Guide for Observing and

Noting Reading Behaviors in the *Assessment Forms* book and CD-ROM is a learning tool in itself; it focuses attention on critical reading behaviors. *The Continuum of Literacy Learning: A Guide to Teaching* is the foundation for instruction; you will be able to make a direct link from the data gathered with the assessment to the continuum's specific behaviors to notice, teach, and support in every instructional context related to literacy. The *Professional Development* DVD is another rich resource; it is designed to help you conduct efficient and effective assessments, learn how to interpret the results, and connect your understandings to instruction. Over time, observations made through the assessment, instruction designed to move the student ahead from level to level, and follow-up assessment will deepen your understanding of literacy development.

How can the Fountas and Pinnell Benchmark Assessment System help upper-grade teachers learn about the reading process?

If you are an upper-grade teacher, you will find that Benchmark Assessment is the perfect starting point for learning to observe and code the reading behaviors of your students. The procedures supported by the Assessment Forms and the analysis training in the Assessment Guide and on the *Professional Development* DVD will help you observe and talk about your students' effective and ineffective behaviors and how the texts they are reading may be appropriate or inappropriate for supporting new learning. After a few months' experience with Benchmark Assessment conferences, you will become much more knowledgeable and interested in what your students are learning about the reading process and become increasingly effective at differentiating instruction.

Is there a place we can pose questions and get a response?

You can post your questions at www.fountas andpinnellbenchmarkassessment.com.

Administering the Assessment

How do you know at which level to start Benchmark Assessment so as to make the administration as time efficient as possible?

We provide several time-saving options. If you have no information on the student's previous reading, the Where-to-Start Word Test provides a rough starting level for assessment and will cut down the number of books a student needs to read before you can identify an independent and an instructional level. If you do have information about a student's previous reading performance, we provide several charts in the Assessment Guide that help determine the starting point by looking at the texts students are reading.

How can I ensure that I am conducting the assessment in a standardized manner?

The precise steps of the assessment conference are described in the Assessment Guide and systematically presented on the Recording Form for each book. The introduction is standardized and printed on the cover of the book as well as on the Recording Form. The steps of the administration, the scoring, and the analysis are all standardized. In addition, the tools supporting the assessment—the F&P Calculator/Stopwatch and the At-a-Glance charts (Assessment at-a-Glance and Coding and Scoring at-a-Glance)—provide an easy way to maintain consistency and help you internalize the steps. Further, the *Professional Development* DVD provides clear examples and plentiful practice opportunities for developing precision and consistency throughout assessment conferences.

Should I administer the assessment to a student who speaks very little English?

We suggest that you follow your school policy regarding the assessment of students whose first language is not English. If you would administer other standardized tests to those students, then you should administer this one. You will find that the gradient of texts will allow most children at least to begin to engage in the reading process.

Can I show the child the pictures during the introduction of the text?

Do not show the pictures during the introduction. The student may look at the front cover as you read the introduction. It is important to follow the standardized directions for the administration so your results will be consistent.

Why do we assess the child on a "cold" reading?

On a cold reading, with only a minimal introduction, you have the best opportunity to observe what the reader can do independently. It is important to have this information in order to guide the reader in his or her independent choices and to determine what the reader needs to learn next.

Why is the introduction so short? Why can't I tell the child more about the text?

Because you want to learn what the child can do independently, it is important not to tell him too much about the text in advance of reading. The introduction is scripted so that the assessment can be as standardized as possible. This standardization is necessary so that we can interpret the results for a class or a school of students.

Oral Reading

Is it permissible for the child to point and read the text?

Instruct the child to point under the words at Levels A and B. After that you do not tell the child to point or not to point. If a child is pointing beyond level C, you may want to make a note of it, as it is likely interfering with fluent, phrased reading.

What if I can't keep up with the coding and I miss some of the student errors?

If you find you cannot keep up with the coding, ask the student to stop until you catch up. The more experienced you get in administering the assessment, the faster your coding will go.

If the student is reading a text that is very hard, is it necessary for him to finish the text so I can determine accuracy level?

No, you can stop the reading early. You will want to say, "This is a very tricky story. You can stop there." As a teacher, you have gathered the data you need and you can discontinue the testing. There is no need to have the student continue to read if the accuracy rate has gone well below 90% for Levels A–K or 95% for Levels L–Z.

When I am assessing and the first book the student reads is too hard, what should I do?

You should judge how hard the book is and move down at least a couple of levels so you can find the easy level and the instructional level.

When I am assessing a student, can I skip levels?

Of course you can skip levels. Your goal is to have the student read the fewest number of books that will give you the data you need as efficiently as possible. If you find a text is very easy, you may want to skip a level or more to get to one that is closer to instructional level. The same applies when a text is very hard and you need to find an instructional level; in this case you may want to skip down some levels.

The directions sometimes indicate the student should continue to read the text silently; wouldn't it be better if I listened to the student read the whole book?

No. It is important to give the student the opportunity to process the text without the oral reinforcement. The oral reading also slows the reader down.

At what level should I expect the student to read fluently?

You should expect the student to read with phrasing and fluency as soon as the early reading behaviors are well under control. We expect the behaviors to be well under control at about the end of Level B or beginning of Level C in instruction. Readers will not be reading fast with complete fluency at the early levels because they are still learning ways of processing print. You should expect, though, to see some phrasing, especially on texts that have dialogue.

Should the child who is reading Level A and B read fluently?

No, you want the child to slow down his language to read one word at a time. At these levels the child is learning to match one spoken word with one printed word. Slow, careful pointing and reading is what you are helping the child control.

Is fluency a stage of reading?

No. Fluency is not a stage of reading. After about level C, readers can read with phrasing and fluency at every level if it is within instructional or independent range.

Do I have to calculate the oral reading rate?

We recommend calculating reading rate only at levels J and above. We have provided you with a formula for calculating reading rate on the Recording Form. You may also use the F & P Calculator/Stopwatch provided with this assessment system to get a quick and accurate score.

Is rate an important factor when children are just beginning to learn to read?

We suggest that you begin to notice the reading rate at about the beginning of grade 2 as one indicator of fluency.

What is the appropriate oral reading rate for each level?

We have provided ranges for reading rate. See the table on page 39.

Why is reading rate important?

Reading rate is one indicator of whether the reader is putting groups of words together in processing the text. When a student is reading one word at a time, the reading gets bogged down and the student is not likely to be able to attend to the meaning of the text.

Comprehension Conversation

Can a child look back at the text during the comprehension conversation?

Though you should not instruct the student to do so, it is permissible for the child to initiate looking back in the text. If the student begins to read the text, ask him to tell the response in his own words.

What happens if the child has to refer back to the text to answer a question? Does this affect his comprehension score?

If a child initiates looking back in the text, locates the information, and provides a correct response, you should give credit for the answer.

Looking back in the text will not affect the comprehension score unless the child is simply pointing at or rereading some of the text to you. Then say, "Tell me in your own words."

What if the child does not understand the question?

Be sure to rephrase the question until the child understands it. Your goal is to determine whether the student understood the information in the story, not whether the student understood the question.

How can I keep up with the note taking?

After you have administered the conversation one or two times, you will be able to interpret the student's comments and connect them to the "key understandings" in the first column. Check the ones the student has covered and take notes only on the additional information provided by the student (if any). Also, you can take a quick moment to make these checks right after the conversation (while the student is writing or after she leaves).

What should I do if the student does not come up with the key understandings?

You can use the probes or questions to elicit answers. You do not need to score the student lower because you had to probe for answers. Some children are not accustomed to spontaneously talking about their thinking, yet they may understand the text very well and demonstrate it when questioned.

Should I "count" the "right answers" the student makes in order to come up with the comprehension score?

No. These texts vary and have different requirements in terms of key understandings (thinking within, beyond, and about the text). Look at the rubric for scoring each category (within, beyond, and about). Make a holistic decision as to the extent to which the student has demonstrated thinking.

Where can I find more information about thinking within, beyond, and about the text?

You will find very detailed descriptions in *Teaching for Comprehending and Fluency: Thinking, Talking, and Writing About Reading, K–8* by Fountas and Pinnell (Heinemann, 2006).

How can I make the comprehension conversation sound "natural"?

You will find some suggestions on page 32 of this guide.

Interpreting & Reporting Results

What if the student achieves instructional or independent level at two levels?

Occasionally you will find that a student performs the same on two levels of text. Use the *higher* of the levels as your indicator.

What if a student reads a text at the instructional level and then a higher level (harder) text at the independent level?

You will want to have the student try another more difficult text to see if the independent level was achieved because the topic was easy. If this text is hard for the student, you will probably want to begin at the original instructional level. If this text is easy for the student, continue until you find another instructional level and begin there. When you begin teaching, you will have the opportunity to observe the reader closely with other texts and can always move up or down a level and change groups if needed.

Does the student's guided reading group have to be at her instructional level?

No. The "Recommended Placement Level," which is the recommended level for guided reading, may be a level lower or higher, depending on your analysis. Pages 44 to 48 describe the thinking process involved in finding a placement level.

What if I have students on six or seven different placement levels? Should I have that many guided reading groups?

It is very difficult to have a large number of reading groups. It makes it hard for you to provide instruction to students on a regular basis because you certainly cannot see all groups every day or even over a week. As you look over your Recommended Placement Levels, you may have to put students who have different instructional levels in a single group. Try to vary your interactions within the group accordingly, giving some students more support and others more challenge (for example, with writing). Most teachers find it difficult to work with more than four or five groups.

What if I have a student who is so far ahead of the class that he doesn't belong in any group?

This kind of student can enjoy participating with the fastest progress group because he will benefit from discussion with others and there is always something more to learn. Advanced readers often read books that are easy for them. Remember that these groups are dynamic, so you can always invite the student to participate in reading some texts and not others. In addition, you will want to provide challenging independent reading for the student (extended through individual conferences).

What if I have a student who reads far above grade level (for example, a first grader who reads level O)?

Look carefully at the comprehension. Chances are, this student has literal comprehension, but lacks rich understanding. Another factor to consider is stamina. The student may be able to read and even have minimal understanding of a high level text; however, it may not be a good experience for her to plow through long chapter books on a regular basis. In general, students enjoy age-appropriate material, so you can extend this student by providing texts just one or two grade levels above her present one. There are always a few students who are truly exceptional, and for those readers you have to make individual decisions.

What if I have a student who reads at a level far below the rest of the students?

This student needs intervention to make accelerated progress, so the first thing to do is to try to get some extra services. At the same time, this student desperately needs classroom instruction, so you should try not to remove him from all of the teaching you are providing. If at all possible, provide enough individual support that the student can participate in a group and can make better progress.

What if I have a student who reads a level with accuracy and understanding but is not at all fluent? Should I go down a level for instruction?

You might want to go down a level, but that is not always the answer. Some students have developed a habit of reading dysfluently and might do so even at easy levels. You'll want to look in greater depth at the student's reading. We suggest using the Six Dimensions Fluency Rubric in the *Assessment Forms* book and CD-ROM so that you can decide with more precision what to teach the student. Sometimes, if accuracy and understanding are there, you can teach intensively for fluency and get a shift in a short time.

How will I know how assessment level relates to our standards for grade level performance in our district?

Your school and your district should make decisions about expected grade level standards, taking into account your state goals. You can refer to our Text Gradient chart (see page 2) for suggested indicators, but adjust them if you have rationales for a different standard.

How can we use the Benchmark Assessment data to improve our school?

Have regular faculty meetings to examine the data within and across grade levels. Look at the general reading levels of the age cohort, but don't stop there. Use the case examples in the guide to help you think about some priorities for teaching students. Think across the language and literacy framework. You can teach for comprehending through interactive read aloud, minilessons, guided reading, and literature discussion. Use *The Continuum of Literacy Learning: A Guide to Teaching* in the benchmark system to find teaching goals.

How can I pass information along to ensure that my students' literacy growth will be documented across the years?

You will find a variety of tools in the Benchmark Assessment package to support the documentation of a student's growth over time as well as ways to track development of whole groups. The *Assessment Forms* CD-ROM provides several options for reports on an individual or the whole class in report or graph format; the *Data Management* CD-ROM makes this even easier. The Student Folder also provides a longitudinal graph for teachers to record progress each year. The folder is designed to be passed from teacher to teacher, from one grade to the next, and to hold the assessment information on one student across nine years, from kindergarten to grade 8.

Is there a way for our school's Benchmark Assessment data to be linked to the district office?

Yes. Heinemann provides an option for districts to link school data to the central office data system.

Glossary

▶ **A**

Accuracy (as in oral reading) or **accuracy rate** The percentage of words the student reads aloud correctly

Analyzing a reading record Looking at errors, self-corrections, and sources of information to plan instruction

Annual Record of Reading Progress A graph showing a student's progress through reading levels across one grade or year; located in *Assessment Forms*

Appeal (in benchmark reading assessment) A reader's verbal or nonverbal request for help

Assessment at-a-Glance A chart containing a brief summary of the steps in administering the Benchmark Assessment (see inside front cover and *Assessment Forms*)

Assessment conference A one-on-one teacher-student Benchmark Assessment session

Assessment Summary The Benchmark Assessment form that combines the results of multiple benchmark book readings from the Recording Forms and guides identification of Benchmark Independent, Benchmark Instructional, and Recommended Placement levels; located in *Assessment Forms*

▶ **B**

Basal reading program A multigrade series, usually of textbook anthologies, with an established scope and sequence of skills

Benchmark Book The leveled text a student reads during Benchmark Assessment

Bi-annual Assessment Summary A form that compiles Assessment Summary results from assessment conferences conducted two times during a school year; located in *Assessment Forms*

▶ **C**

Class Record A chart containing a class list on which to record students' independent and/or instructional levels in order to see a group's reading levels in relation to each other; located in *Assessment Forms*

Code (a reading record) Using a copy of the benchmark text, you record a student's oral reading errors, self-corrections, and other behaviors

Coding and Scoring Errors at-a-Glance A chart containing a brief summary of how to code and score oral reading errors (see inside back cover and *Assessment Forms*)

Comprehension (as in reading) The process of constructing meaning while reading a text

Comprehension conversation Part Two of the Benchmark Assessment in which the student shares his understanding of the text

Core reading program (see basal reading program)

▶ **D**

Diagnostic assessment A reading assessment designed to identify strengths and weaknesses in knowledge of specific language elements

▶ **E**

Error A reader's response that is not consistent with the text and that is *not* self-corrected

▶ **F**

F & P Calculator/Stopwatch A device that will calculate the reading time, reading rate, accuracy rate, and self-correction ratio for a reading

Fiction A story created from the imagination

Fluency (as in reading) The way an oral reading sounds, including phrasing, intonation, pausing, stress, rate, and integration of the first five factors

Font The style and size of type (alphabet characters) in a printed piece

▶ **G**

Genre A category of texts that share a particular form, common attributes, or content

Gradient of reading difficulty (see text gradient)

Guide for Observing and Noting Reading Behaviors Lists questions a teacher should ask himself or herself about the ways a student is processing or problem solving texts; located in *Assessment Forms*

▶ **H**

Hard reading level The level at which the student reads the text aloud with less than 90% accuracy (levels A–K) or less than 95% accuracy (levels L–Z)

Holistic scoring A score that reflects overall performance rather than counting items

▶ **I**

Independent reading level The level at which the student reads the text with 95% or higher accuracy and excellent or satisfactory comprehension (levels A–K) or 98% or higher accuracy with excellent or satisfactory comprehension (levels L–Z)

Individual instruction The teacher working with one student

Insertion (as in error in reading) A word added during oral reading that is not in the text

Instructional reading level At levels A–K, he level at which the student reads the text with 90–94% accuracy and excellent or satisfactory comprehension; or 95% or higher accuracy and limited comprehension. At levels L–Z, the level at which the student reads the text with 95–97% accuracy and excellent or satisfactory comprehension; or 98% or higher accuracy and limited comprehension.

Interactive read-aloud The teacher reading aloud to a group of students and inviting them to think and talk about the text before, during, and after reading

Intervention Intensive additional instruction for students not progressing as rapidly as expected; usually one-on-one tutoring or small-group (one-on-three) teaching

▶ **K**

Key understandings (in benchmark books) Important ideas within (literal), beyond (implied), or about (determined through critical analysis) the text that are necessary to comprehension

▶ **L**

Leveled books Texts designated along a gradient from level A (easiest) to level Z (hardest)

Literature discussion Students talking to each other about a text, either in a small group or with the whole class

Longitudinal Record of Reading Progress A graph showing a student's progress through reading levels across multiple grades; located in *Assessment Forms* book and CD-ROM and on Student Folders

▶ **M**

M (meaning) One of three sources of information that readers use (MSV: meaning, language structure, visual information). Meaning, the semantic system of language, refers to meaning derived from words, meaning across a text or texts, and meaning from personal experience or knowledge.

Minilesson A brief, focused lesson on any aspect of reading or writing, usually involving the whole class or a small group

▶ **N**

Nonfiction A text whose primary purpose is to convey information and facts that are accurate

▶ **O**

Omission (as in error) A word left out or skipped during oral reading

Optional assessments A selection of Phonics and Word Analysis plus Vocabulary Assessments designed to target specific areas of literacy knowledge; located in *Assessment Forms* book and CD-ROM

Oral reading (in Benchmark Assessment) Part II of the Benchmark Assessment during which the student reads a text aloud while the teacher codes the reading

▶ **P**

Phonics The study and teaching of letters and their related sounds as they function within words

Phonics and Word Analysis Assessments A set of optional assessments that evaluates letter knowledge, early literacy concepts, high-frequency words, phonological awareness, letter-sound relationships, and word structure; located in *Assessment Forms* book and CD-ROM

Preprimer A beginning text used to teach reading; usually the first books read in a basal reading program

Primer An early reading text; follows preprimers and precedes the grade 1 text in a basal reading program

Processing (as in reading) The mental operations involved in constructing meaning from written language

Prompt (in Benchmark Assessment) A question, direction, or statement designed to encourage the student to say more about a topic during a comprehension conversation

▶ **Q**

Quarterly Assessment Summary A form that compiles Assessment Summary results from assessment conferences conducted four times during a school year; located in *Assessment Forms* book and CD-ROM

▶ **R**

Reading graph A graph that charts a student or students' progress through leveled books (see the Annual Record of Reading Progress and the Longitudinal Record of Reading Progress)

Reading interview An optional assessment containing questions to gain information about a student's reading preferences and reading history; located in *Assessment Forms* book and CD-ROM

Reading Rate (WPM) The number of words a student reads per minute, either orally (as in Benchmark Assessment) or silently

Reading record (in Benchmark Assessment) The transcript of the text on which oral reading is coded

Recording Form The form on which oral reading, the comprehension conversation, and the writing about reading assessment for a text are coded and scored. There is a Recording Form for each book in the Benchmark Assessment System. All are located in *Assessment Forms* book and CD-ROM.

Recommended Placement level The level the teacher, after taking into consideration all data gathered through Benchmark Assessment, decides is appropriate for reading instruction

Repetition (in oral reading) The reader saying a word, phrase, or section of the text more than once

Rubric A scoring tool that relies on descriptions of response categories for evaluation

Running words (in Benchmark Assessment) The number of words read aloud and coded during Part One Oral Reading

▶ **S**

S (structure) One of three sources of information that readers use (MSV: meaning, language structure, visual information). Language structure refers to the way words are put together in phrases and sentences (syntax or grammar).

Scoring and Analysis at-a-Glance A brief summary of the steps in scoring the three parts of a Benchmark Assessment: oral reading, comprehension conversation, and writing about reading; located in *Assessment Forms* book and CD-ROM

Scoring a reading record (in Benchmark Assessment) Counting coded errors and self-corrections, which allows you to calculate *accuracy rate* and *self-correction ratio* on the Recording Form. The Form also provides space for a general *fluency score* (levels C–N) and *reading rate* (levels J–N).

Searching The reader looking for information in order to read accurately, self-correct, or understand a text

Self-correction ratio The proportion of errors the reader corrects himself

Shared and performance reading The teacher and students reading together (or in parts) a text that they know well

Silent reading The reader reading the text to herself

Six Dimensions Fluency Rubric A rubric for evaluating oral reading fluency on six dimensions: pausing, phrasing, stress, intonation, rate, and the combination of these, integration; located in *Assessment Forms* book and CD-ROM

Small-group reading instruction The teacher working with students brought together because they are similar enough in reading development to teach in a small group; guided reading

Sounding out (in Benchmark Reading Assessment) Pronouncing the sounds of the letters in a word as a step in reading the word

Spelling aloud (in Benchmark Reading Assessment) Naming the letters in a word rather than reading the word

Standardized Remaining essentially the same across multiple instances

Substitution (as in error in reading) The reader reading aloud one (incorrect) word for another

▶ **T**

Text gradient A twenty-six-point (A–Z) text-rating scale of difficulty in which each text level, from the easiest at level A to the most challenging at level Z, represents a small but significant increase in difficulty over the previous level. The gradient correlates these levels to grade levels.

Told (in Benchmark Reading Assessment) The teacher telling the reader a word he cannot read

Tri-annual Assessment Summary A form that compiles Assessment Summary results from assessment conferences conducted three times during a school year; located in *Assessment Forms* book and CD-ROM

▶ **V**

V (visual information) One of three sources of information that readers use (MSV: meaning, language structure, visual information). Visual information refers to the letters that represent the sounds of language and way they are combined (spelling patterns) to create words; visual information at the sentence level includes punctuation.

Vocabulary Words and their meanings

Vocabulary Assessments A set of optional assessments that evaluates a student's word knowledge (concept words, vocabulary in context), understanding of word relationships (synonyms, antonyms, roots, analogies), and ability to derive the precise meaning of words in the context of a short book (vocabulary in context); located in *Assessment Forms* book and CD-ROM

▶ **W**

Where-to-Start Word Test A graded list of increasingly difficult words. The number of words the student reads aloud accurately is converted into an approximate level for beginning Benchmark Assessment. Located in *Assessment Forms* book and CD-ROM.

Whole-group instruction The teacher teaching a lesson to an entire class or a large part of it

Writing Students engaging in the writing process and producing pieces of their own writing in many genres

Writing about reading Students responding to reading a text by writing and sometimes drawing

▶ **Y**

You Try It (in Benchmark Reading Assessment) A teacher prompt that directs a student to make an attempt at reading a word during oral reading